THE FINAL WEEK OF JESUS

FOR MY FATHER- AND MOTHER-IN-LAW

Charles and Romadene Preston

FOR GIVING ME SUCH DELIGHT

THE FINAL
WEEK OF JESUS

Highlights from And the Angels Were Silent

Illustrated by Keith Criss

MAX LUCADO

MULTNOMAH BOOKS

Text for *The Final Week of Jesus*
taken from *And the Angels Were Silent.*

Other books by Max Lucado include:
On the Anvil, Six Hours One Friday
No Wonder They Call Him the Savior, The Applause of Heaven
God Came Near, In the Eye of the Storm

Edited by Liz Heaney and Carol Bartley
Design by David Uttley

THE FINAL WEEK OF JESUS
© 1994 by Max Lucado
Illustrations © 1994 by Keith Criss, All Rights Reserved
Published by Multnomah Publishers, Inc.

International Standard Book Number: 0-88070-630-9 (hardback)
International Standard Book Number: 1-57673-728-4 (paperback)

Printed in the United States of America.

LIBRARY OF CONGRESS CATALOGING-IN-PUBLICATION DATA
Lucado, Max.
The Final Week of Jesus / Max Lucado ; illustrated by Keith Criss,
p. cm.

1.Jesus Christ - - Biography - - Passion Week - - 2.Christ - - Biography - -
Devotional literature.
I. Title.

BT 414.L83 1994   94-128
232.96 - - dc20   CIP

99 00 01 02 03 — 10 9 8 7 6 5

Contents

Tuesday

Thursday

Friday

Sunday

A WORD BEFORE

*I*t's early in the final week. The props and players for Friday's drama are in position. Six-inch spikes are in the bin. A crossbeam leans against a shed wall. Thorn limbs are wrapped around a trellis awaiting the weaving of a soldier's fingers.

The players are nearing the stage. Pilate is concerned at the number of Passover pilgrims. Annas and Caiaphas are restless over a volatile Nazarene. Judas views his master with furtive eyes. A centurion is available, awaiting the next crucifixions.

Players and props. Only this is no play, it's a divine plan. A plan begun before Adam felt heaven's breath and now all heaven waits and watches. All eyes are on one figure—the Nazarene.

Commonly clad. Uncommonly focused. Leaving Jericho and walking toward Jerusalem. He doesn't chatter. He doesn't pause. He is on a journey. His final journey.

Even the angels are silent. They know this is no ordinary walk. They know this is no ordinary week. For hinged on this week is the door of eternity.

Let's walk with him.

Let's see how Jesus spent his final days.

Let's see what mattered to God.

When a man knows the end is near—only the important surfaces. Impending death distills the vital. The trivial is bypassed. The unnecessary is overlooked. That which is vital remains. So, if you would know Christ, ponder his final days.

He knew the end was near. He knew the finality of Friday. He read the last chapter before it was written and heard the final chorus before it was sung. As a result, the critical was centrifuged from the casual. Distilled truths taught. Deliberate deeds done. Each step calculated. Every act premeditated.

Knowing he had just one week with the disciples, what did Jesus tell them? Knowing it would be his last time in the temple, how did he act? Conscious that the last sand was slipping through the hourglass, what mattered?[1]

Enter the holy week and observe.

Feel his passion. Laughing as children sing. Weeping as Jerusalem ignores. Scorning as priests accuse. Pleading as disciples sleep. Feeling sad as Pilate turns.

Sense his power. Blind eyes . . . seeing. Fruitless tree . . . withering. Money changers . . . scampering. Religious leaders . . . cowering. Tomb . . . opening.

Hear his promise. Death has no power. Failure holds no prisoners. Fear has no control. For God has come, God has come into your world . . . to take you home.

Let's follow Jesus on his final journey. For by observing his, we may learn how to make ours.

Friday

CHAPTER ONE

TOO LITTLE,
TOO LATE, TOO GOOD TO BE TRUE

*G*od has a peculiar passion for the forgotten. Have you noticed?

See his hand on the festered skin of the leper?

See the face of the prostitute cupped in his hands?

Notice how he responds to the touch of the woman with the hemorrhage?

See him with his arm around little Zacchaeus?

Over and over again God wants us to get the message: He has a peculiar passion for the forgotten. What society puts out, God puts in. What the world writes off, God picks up. That must be why Jesus told the story of the chosen workers. It's the first story of his final week. It's the last story he will tell before entering Jerusalem. Once inside the city walls Jesus becomes a marked man. The hourglass will be turned and the final countdown and chaos will begin.

"Those who have the last place now will have the first place in the future."
MATTHEW 20:16

But it's not Jerusalem. And he's not addressing his enemies. It's the Jericho countryside and he's with friends. And for them he weaves this parable of grace.

A certain landowner needs workers. At 6:00 A.M. he picks his crew, they agree on a wage, and he puts them to work. At 9:00 he is back at the unemployment agency and picks a few more. At noon he is back and at

3:00 in the afternoon he is back and at 5:00, you guessed it. He's back again.

Now, the punchline of the story is the anger the twelve-hour laborers felt when the other guys got the same wage. That's a great message, but we'll save it for another book.

I want to home in on an often forgotten scene in the story: the choosing. Can you see it? It happened at 9:00. It happened at noon. It happened at 3:00. But most passionately, it happened at 5:00.

Five in the afternoon. Tell me. What is a worker still doing in the yard at 5:00 in the afternoon? The best have long since gone. The mediocre workers went at lunch. The last string went at 3:00. What kind of worker is left at 5:00 P.M.?

All day they get passed by. They are unskilled. Untrained. Uneducated. They are hanging with one hand from the bottom of the ladder. They are absolutely dependent upon a merciful boss giving them a chance they don't deserve.

So, by the way, were we. Lest we get a bit cocky, we might take Paul's advice and look at what we were when God called us.[1] Do you remember?

Some of us were polished and sharp but papier-mâché thin. Others of us didn't even try to hide our despair. We drank it. We smelled it. We shot it. We sold it. Life was a passion-pursuit. We were on a treasure hunt for an empty chest in a dead-end canyon.

Do you remember how you felt? Do you remember the perspiration on your forehead and the crack in your soul? Do you remember how you tried to hide the loneliness until it got bigger than you and then you just tried to survive?

Hold that picture for a moment. Now answer this. Why did he choose you? Why did he choose me? Honestly. Why? What do we have that he needs?

Intellect? Do we honestly think for one minute that we have—or ever will have—a thought he hasn't had?

Willpower? I can respect that. Some of us are stubborn enough to walk on water if we felt called to do so . . . but to think God's kingdom would have done a belly-up without our determination?

How about money? We came into the kingdom with a nice little nest egg. Perhaps that's why we were chosen. Perhaps the creator of heaven and earth could use a little of our cash. Maybe the owner of every breath and every person and the author of history was getting low on capital and he saw us and our black ink and . . .

Get the point?

We were chosen for the same reason the five o'clock workers were. You and me? We are the five o'clock workers.

Why did he pick you? He wanted to. After all, you are his. He made you. He brought you home. He owns you. And once upon a time, he tapped you on the shoulder and reminded you of that fact. No matter how long you'd waited or how much time you'd wasted, you are his and he has a place for you.

FROM JERICHO TO JERUSALEM

*I*f you want to know someone's heart, observe that person's final journey.

The story of young Matthew Huffman came across my desk the week I was writing this chapter. He was the six-year-old son of missionaries in Salvador, Brazil. One morning he began to complain of fever. As his temperature went up, he began losing his eyesight. His mother and father put him in the car and raced him to the hospital.

As they were driving and he was lying on his mother's lap, he did something his parents will never forget. He extended his hand in the air. His mother took it and he pulled it away. He extended it again. She again took it and he, again, pulled it back and reached into the air. Confused, the mother asked her son, "What are you reaching for, Matthew?"

"I'm reaching for Jesus' hand," he answered. And with those words he closed his eyes and slid into a coma from which he never would awaken. He died two days later, a victim of bacterial meningitis.

Of all the things he didn't learn in his short life, he'd learned the most important: who to reach for in the hour of death.

You can tell a lot about a person by the way he dies.

With Jesus' mission before him, he stopped his disciples and told them for the third time of his conclusive encounter with the enemy. "We are going to Jerusalem. The Son of Man will be turned over to the leading priests and the teachers of the law, and they will say that he must die. They will give the Son of Man to the non-Jewish people to laugh at him and beat him with whips and crucify him. But on the third day he will be raised to life again."[1]

Note his detailed knowledge of the event. He tells who—"the leading priests and teachers of the law." He tells what—"they will give the Son of Man to the non-Jewish people to laugh at him and beat him with whips and crucify him." He tells when—"but on the third day he will be raised to life again."

Forget any suggestion that Jesus was trapped. Erase any theory that Jesus made a miscalculation. Ignore any speculation that the cross was a last-ditch attempt to salvage a dying mission.

For if these words tell us anything, they tell us that Jesus died . . . on purpose. No surprise. No hesitation. No faltering.

> "They will give the Son of Man to the non-Jewish people to laugh at him and beat him with whips and crucify him. But on the third day, he will be raised to life again."
>
> MATTHEW 20:19

You can tell a lot about a person by the way he dies. And the way Jesus marched to his death leaves no doubt: he had come to earth for this moment. Read the words of Peter. "Jesus was given to you, and with the help of those who don't know the law, you put him to death by nailing him to a cross. But this was God's plan which he had made long ago; he knew all this would happen."[2]

No, the journey to Jerusalem didn't begin in Jericho. It didn't begin in Galilee. It didn't begin in Nazareth. It didn't even begin in Bethlehem.

The journey to the cross began long before. As the echo of the crunching of the fruit was still sounding in the garden, Jesus was leaving for Calvary.

Jesus stepped toward Jerusalem with the promise of God in his heart. The divinity of Christ assured the humanity of Christ, and Jesus spoke loud enough for the pits of hell to vibrate: "But on the third day he will be raised to life again."

Is there a Jerusalem on your horizon? Are you a brief journey away from painful encounters? Are you only steps away from the walls of your own heartache?

Learn a lesson from your master. Don't march into battle with the enemy without first claiming the courage from God's promises. May I give you a few examples?

When you are confused: " 'I know what I am planning for you,' says the LORD. 'I have good plans for you, not plans to hurt you.' "³

If you feel weighted by yesterday's failures: "So now, those who are in Christ Jesus are not judged guilty."⁴

On those nights when you wonder where God is: "I am the Holy One, and I am among you."⁵

If you think you can fall beyond God's love: "Understand the greatness of Christ's love—how wide and how long and how high and how deep that love is. Christ's love is greater than anyone can ever know."⁶

Next time you find yourself on a Jericho road marching toward Jerusalem, put the promises of God on your lips.

Eighteen

The Sacrificial General

he decision had been made. The troops had been deployed and the battleships were on their way. Nearly three million soldiers were preparing to slam against Hitler's Atlantic wall in France. D-Day was set in motion. Responsibility for the invasion fell squarely on the four-starred shoulders of General Dwight D. Eisenhower.

The general spent the night before the attack with the men of the 101st Airborne. They called themselves The Screaming Eagles. As his men prepared their planes and checked their equipment, Ike went from soldier to soldier offering words of encouragement. Many of the flyers were young enough to be his sons. He treated them as if they were. A correspondent wrote that as Eisenhower watched the C-47s take off and disappear into the darkness, his hands were sunk deeply into his pockets and his eyes were full of tears.

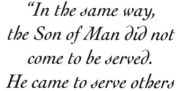

"In the same way, the Son of Man did not come to be served. He came to serve others and to give his life as a ransom for many people."

MATTHEW 20:28

The general then went to his quarters and sat at his desk. He took a pen and paper and wrote a message—a message which would be delivered to the White House in the event of a defeat.

It was as brief as it was courageous. "Our landings . . . have failed . . . the troops, the Air, and the Navy did all that bravery and devotion to duty could do. If any blame or fault attaches itself to the attempt it was mine alone."[1]

It could be argued that the greatest act of courage that day was not in a cockpit or foxhole, but at a desk when the one at the top took responsibility for the ones below. When the one in charge took the blame—even before the blame needed to be taken.

Rare leader, this general. Unusual, this display of courage. He modeled a quality seldom seen in our society of lawsuits, dismissals, and divorces. Most of us are willing to take credit for the good we do. Some are willing to take the rap for the bad we do. But few will assume responsibilities for the mistakes of others. Still fewer will shoulder the blame for mistakes yet uncommitted.

Eisenhower did. As a result, he became a hero.

Jesus did. As a result, he's our Savior.

Before the war began, he forgave. Before a mistake could be made, for-giveness was offered. Before blame could be given, grace was provided.

The one at the top took responsibility for the ones at the bottom. Read how Jesus describes what he came to do.

"The Son of Man did not come to be served. He came to serve others and to give his life as a ransom for many people."[2]

The phrase "Son of Man" conjured the same images for the Jew of Christ's era that the title "general" creates for you and me. It was a state-ment of authority and power.

Consider all the titles Jesus could have used to define himself on earth: King of kings, the great I AM, the Beginning and the End, the Lord of All, Jehovah, High and Holy. All of these and a dozen others would have been appropriate.

But Jesus didn't use them.

Instead, he called himself the Son of Man. This title appears eighty-two times in the New Testament. Eighty-one of which are in the Gospels. Eighty of which are directly from the lips of Jesus.

To the Jew the Son of Man was a symbol of triumph. The conqueror. The equalizer. The score-settler. The big brother. The intimidator. The Starship *Enterprise*. The right arm of the High and Holy. The king who roared down from the heavens in a fiery chariot of vengeance and anger toward those who have oppressed God's holy people.[3]

The Son of Man was the four-starred general who called his army to invade and led his troops to victory.

For that reason when Jesus spoke of the Son of Man in terms of power, the people cheered.

When he spoke of a new world where the Son of Man would sit on his glorious throne[4], the people understood.

When he spoke of the Son of Man who would come on the clouds of heaven with great power and authority[5], the people could envision the scene.

When he spoke of the Son of Man seated at the right hand of power[6], everyone could imagine the picture.

But what's this he's saying? "The Son of Man did not come to be served. He came to serve others." Earlier he'd told them, "The Son of Man will be handed over to people, and they will kill him. After three days, he will rise from the dead."[7]

Wait a minute! That's an impossible, incredible, intolerable contradiction of terms. No wonder "the followers did not understand what Jesus meant, and they were afraid to ask him."[8] The king who came to serve? The Son of Man being betrayed? The Conqueror—killed? The Ambassador of the Ancient of Days—mocked? Spit upon?

But such is the irony of Jesus wearing the title "the Son of Man." It is also the irony of the cross. Calvary is a hybrid of God's lofty status and his deep devotion. The thunderclap which echoed when God's sovereignty collided with his love. The marriage of heaven's kingship and heaven's compassion.[9] The very instrument of the cross is symbolic, the vertical beam of holiness intersecting with the horizontal bar of love.

Jesus wears a sovereign crown but bears a father's heart.

He is a general who takes responsibility for his soldiers' mistakes.

But Jesus didn't write a note, he paid the price. He didn't just assume the blame, he seized the sin. He became the ransom. He is the general who dies in the place of the private, the King who suffers for the peasant, the Master who sacrifices himself for the servant.

He is the Son of Man who came to serve and to give his life as a ransom . . . for you.

Saturday

CHAPTER FOUR

DON'T JUST DO SOMETHING, STAND THERE

A couple of weeks ago Andrea and I went on an adventure—on bicycles. She had just learned to keep her balance on a two-wheeler and was ready to leave the safety of the front street and try the hill behind our house. She'd never ridden down a hill before.

We sat atop the descent and looked down it. To her it was Everest. "You sure you want to try?" I asked.

"I think so," she gulped.

"Just put on your brakes when you want to stop. Don't forget your brakes."

"Okay."

I rode to the midway point and waited. Down she came. The bike began to pick up speed. The handlebars began to shake. Her eyes got big. Her pedals moved in a blur. As she raced past she screamed, "I can't remember how to stop pedaling!"

She crashed into the curb.

If you don't know how to stop, the result can be painful. True on bikes. True in life.

Do you remember how to stop?

Ever feel like you're racing downhill on a runaway bike and you don't remember how to brake? Ever feel the wheels of your life racing faster and faster as you speed past the people you love? Could you use a reminder on how to slow it all down?

If so, read what Jesus did during the last Sabbath of his life. Start in the Gospel of Matthew. Didn't find anything? Try Mark. Read what Mark recorded about the way Jesus spent the Sabbath. Nothing there either? Strange. What about Luke? What does Luke say? Not a reference to the day? Not a word about it? Well, try John. Surely John mentions the Sabbath. He doesn't? No reference? Hmmmm. Looks like Jesus was quiet that day.

"Wait a minute. That's it?" That's it.

"You mean with one week left to live, Jesus observed the Sabbath?" As far as we can tell.

"You mean with all those apostles to train and people to teach, he took a day to rest and worship?" Apparently so.

"You're telling me that Jesus thought worship was more important than work?" That's exactly what I'm telling you.

"Work and get everything done during six days each week, but the seventh day is a day of rest to honor the LORD your God."

EXODUS 20:9-10

For such is the purpose of the Sabbath. And such was the practice of Jesus. "On the Sabbath day he went to the synagogue, *as he always did,* and stood up to read."[1] Should we do any less?

If Jesus found time in the midst of a racing agenda to stop the rush and sit in the silence, do you think we could, too?

It's almost as if activity is a sign of maturity. After all, isn't there a beatitude which reads, "Blessed are the busy"? No, there isn't. But there is a verse which summarizes many lives: "Man is a mere phantom as he goes to and fro: He bustles about, but only in vain; he heaps up wealth, not knowing who will get it."[2]

Does that sound like your life? Are you so seldom in one place that your friends regard you as a phantom? Are you so constantly on the move that your family is beginning to question your existence? Do you take pride in your frenzy at the expense of your faith?

Are Andrea's words yours? "I don't remember how to stop." If so, you are headed for a crash.

Slow down. If God commanded it, you need it. If Jesus modeled it, you need it. God still provides the manna. Trust him. Take a day to say no to work and yes to worship.

One final thought.

One of the reference points of London is the Charing Cross. It is near the geographical center of the city and serves as a navigational tool for those confused by the streets.

A little girl was lost in the great city. A policeman found her. Between sobs and tears, she explained she didn't know her way home. He asked her if she knew her address. She didn't. He asked her phone number; she didn't know that either. But when he asked her what she knew, suddenly her face lit up.

"I know the Cross," she said. "Show me the Cross and I can find my way home from there."

So can you. Keep a clear vision of the cross on your horizon and you can find your way home. Such is the purpose of your day of rest: to relax your body, but more importantly to restore your vision. A day in which you get your bearings so you can find your way home.

CHAPTER FIVE

RISKY LOVE

A cluster of friends encircle Jesus. They are at the table. The city is Bethany and the house is Simon's. He was known as Simon the leper. But not any longer. Now he is just Simon. We don't know when Jesus healed him. But we do know what he was like before Jesus healed him. Stooped shoulders. Fingerless hand. Scabbed arm and infected back draped in rags. A tattered wrap which hides all of the face except for two screaming white eyes.

But that was before Jesus' touch. Was Simon the one Jesus healed after he delivered the Sermon on the Mount? Was he the one in the ten who returned to say thank you? Was he one of the four thousand Jesus helped in Bethsaida? Or was he one of the nameless myriads the gospel writers didn't take time to mention?

We don't know. But we know he had Jesus and his disciples over for dinner.

A simple act, but it must have meant a lot to Jesus. After all, the Pharisees are already clearing him a cell on death row. Won't be long until they finger Lazarus as an accomplice. Could be that the whole lot of them will be on wanted posters by the end of the week. It takes nerve

"Mary brought in a pint of very expensive perfume made from pure nard. She poured the perfume on Jesus' feet, and then she wiped his feet with her hair. And the sweet smell from the perfume filled the whole house."

JOHN 12:3

to have a wanted man in your home.

But it takes more nerve to put your hand on a leper's sore.

Simon didn't forget what Jesus had done. He couldn't forget. Where there had been a nub, there was now a finger for his daughter to hold. Where there had been ulcerous sores, there was now skin for his wife to stroke. And where there had been lonely hours in quarantine, there were now happy hours such as this—a house full of friends, a table full of food.

No, Simon didn't forget. Simon knew what it was like to stare death in the face. He knew what it was like to have no home to call your own and he knew what it was like to be misunderstood. He wanted Jesus to know that if he ever needed a meal and a place to lay his head, there was one house in Bethany to which he could go.

Risky love seizes the moment. Simon took a chance. He gave Jesus a good meal. Not much, but more than most. And when the priests accused and the soldiers slapped, perhaps Jesus remembered what Simon did and was strengthened.

And when he remembered Simon's meal, perhaps he remembered Mary's gesture. Maybe he could even smell the perfume. Not unlikely that he could. After all it was twelve ounces. Imported. Concentrated. Sweet. Strong enough to scent a man's clothes for days.

Between the lashings, I wonder, did he relive the moment? As he hugged the Roman post and braced himself for the next ripping of his back, did he remember the oil which soothed his skin? Could he, in the faces of the women who stared, see the small, soft face of Mary, who cared?

Thirty

She was the only one who believed him. Whenever he spoke of his death the others shrugged, the others doubted, but Mary believed. Mary believed because he spoke with a firmness she'd heard before.

"Lazarus, come out!" he'd demanded, and her brother came out. After four days in a stone-sealed grave he walked out.

And as Mary kissed the now-warm hands of her just-dead brother, she turned and looked. Jesus was smiling. Tear streaks were dry and the teeth shone from beneath the beard. He was smiling.

And in her heart she knew she would never doubt his words.

So when he spoke of his death, she believed.

And when she saw the three together, she couldn't resist. Simon, the healed leper, head thrown back in laughter. Lazarus, the resurrected corpse, leaning in to see what Jesus has said. And Jesus, the source of life for both, beginning his joke a second time. "Now is the right time," she told herself.

It wasn't an act of impulse. She'd carried the large vial of perfume from her house to Simon's. It wasn't a spontaneous gesture. But it was an extravagant one. The perfume was worth a year's wages. Maybe the only thing of value she had. It wasn't a logical thing to do, but since when has love been led by logic?

Logic hadn't touched Simon. Common sense hadn't wept at Lazarus's tomb. Practicality didn't feed the crowds or love the children.

Love did. Extravagant, risky, chance-taking love.

And now someone needs to show the same to the giver of such love.

So Mary did. She stepped up behind him and stood with the jar in her hand. Within a couple of moments every mouth was silent and every eye wide as they watched her nervous fingers remove the ornate cover.

Only Jesus was unaware of her presence. Just as he noticed everyone looking behind him, she began to pour. Over his head. Over his shoulders. Down his back. She would have poured herself out for him if she could.

The fragrance rushed through the room. Smells of cooked lamb and herbs were lost in the aroma of the sweet ointment. "Wherever you go," the gesture spoke, "breathe the aroma and remember one who cares."

On his skin the fragrance of faith. In his clothing the balm of belief. Even as the soldiers divided his garments, her gesture brought a bouquet into a cemetery.

The other disciples had mocked her extravagance. They thought it foolish. Ironic. Jesus had saved them from a sinking boat in a stormy sea. He'd enabled them to heal and preach. He'd brought focus into their fuzzy lives. They, the recipients of exorbitant love, chastised her generosity.

Don't miss Jesus' prompt defense of Mary. "Why are you troubling this woman? She has done an excellent thing for me." [1]

Jesus' message is just as powerful today as it was then. Don't miss it: "There is a time for risky love. There is a time for extravagant gestures. There is a time to pour out your affections on one you love. And when the time comes—seize it, don't miss it."

Go to the effort. Invest the time. Write the letter. Make the apology. Take the trip. Purchase the gift. Do it. The seized opportunity renders joy. The neglected brings regret.

The reward was great for Simon. He was privileged to give rest to the one who made the earth. Simon's gesture will never be forgotten.

Neither will Mary's. Jesus promised, "Wherever the Good News is preached in all the world, what this woman has done will be told, and people will remember her." [2]

Simon and Mary: Examples of the risky gift given at the right time.

Sunday

CHAPTER SIX

THE GUY
WITH THE DONKEY

When we all get home I know what I want to do. There's someone I want to get to know. You go ahead and swap stories with Mary or talk doctrine with Paul. I'll catch up with you soon. But first, I want to meet the guy with the donkey.

I don't know his name or what he looks like. I only know one thing: what he gave. He gave a donkey to Jesus on the Sunday he entered Jerusalem.

"Go to the town you can see there. When you enter it, you will quickly find a donkey tied there with its colt. Untie them and bring them to me. If anyone asks you why you are taking the donkeys, say that the Master needs them, and he will send them at once."[1]

When we all get to heaven I want to visit this fellow. I have several questions for him.

How did you know? How did you know it was Jesus who needed a donkey? Did you have a vision? Did you get a telegram? Did an angel appear in your bowl of lentils?

Was it hard to give? Was it difficult to give something to Jesus for him to use? I want to ask that question because sometimes it's hard for me. Sometimes I like to keep my animals to myself. Sometimes when God wants something I act like I don't know he needs it.

How did it feel? How did it feel to look out and see Jesus on the back of the donkey that lived in your barn? Were you proud? Were you surprised? Were you annoyed?

Did you know? Did you have any idea that your generosity would be used for such a noble purpose? Did it ever occur to you that God was going to ride your donkey? Were you aware that all four Gospel writers would tell your story? Did it ever cross your mind that a couple of millenniums later, a curious preacher in South Texas would be pondering your plight late at night?

And as I ponder yours, I ponder mine. Sometimes I get the impression that God wants me to give him something, and sometimes I don't give it because I don't know for sure, and then I feel bad because I've missed my chance. Other times I know he wants something but I don't give it because I'm too selfish. And other times, too few times, I hear him and I obey him and feel honored that a gift of mine would be used to carry Jesus into another place. And still other times I wonder if my little deeds today will make a difference in the long haul.

"If anyone asks you why you are taking the donkeys, say that the Master needs them, and he will send them at once."

MATTHEW 21:3

Maybe you have those questions, too. All of us have a donkey. You and I each have something in our lives, which, if given back to God, could, like the donkey, move Jesus and his story further down the road. Maybe you can sing or hug or program a computer or speak Swahili or write a check.

Whichever, that's your donkey.

Whichever, your donkey belongs to him.

It really does belong to him. Your gifts are his and the donkey was his.

The original wording of the instructions Jesus gave to his disciples is proof: "If anyone asks you why you are taking the donkey, you are to say, 'Its Lord is in need.'"

The language Jesus used is the language of a royal levy. It was an ancient law which required the citizen to render to the king any item or service he or one of his emissaries might request.[2] In making such a request, Jesus is claiming to be king. He is speaking as one in authority. He is stating that as king he has rights to any possession of his subjects.

It could be that God wants to mount your donkey and enter the walls of another city, another nation, another heart. Do you let him? Do you give it? Or do you hesitate?

That guy who gave Jesus the donkey is just one in a long line of folks who gave little things to a big God. Scripture has quite a gallery of donkey-givers. In fact, heaven may have a shrine to honor God's uncommon use of the common.

It's a place you won't want to miss. Stroll through and see Rahab's rope, Paul's bucket, David's sling, and Samson's jawbone. Wrap your hand around the staff which split the sea and smote the rock. Sniff the ointment which soothed Jesus' skin and lifted his heart. Rest your head on the same cloak which gave comfort to Christ in the boat and run your hand along the smooth wood of the manger, soft as a baby's skin. Or set your shoulder beneath the heavy Roman beam, as coarse as a traitor's kiss.

I don't know if these items will be there. But I am sure of one thing—the people who used them will.

Monday

HUCKSTERS AND HYPOCRITES

*S*peedy Morris is the basketball coach for LaSalle University. He was shaving when his wife told him he was wanted on the phone by *Sports Illustrated.* He got so excited over the prospect of national recognition that he hurried his shave and nicked himself. Not wanting to delay the caller, he ran out of the bathroom, lost his balance, and tumbled down the stairs. Limping, with blood and lather on his face, he finally got to the phone.

"Sports Illustrated?" he panted.

Imagine Morris's disappointment when the voice on the other end droned, "Yes it is, and for seventy-five cents an issue you can get a year's subscription. . . ." [1]

It's tough to be let down. It's disappointing when you think someone is interested in you, only to find he is interested in your money. When sales people do it, it's irritating—but when people of faith do it, it can be devastating.

It's a sad but true fact of the faith: religion is used for profit and prestige. When it is there are two results: people are exploited and God is infuriated.

There's no better example of this than what happened at the temple. After he had entered the city on the back of a donkey, Jesus "went into the temple. After he had looked at everything, since it was already late, he went out to Bethany with the twelve apostles."[2]

Did you catch that? The first place Jesus went when he arrived in Jerusalem was the temple. He'd just been paraded through the streets and treated like a king. It was Sunday, the first day of the Passover week. Hundreds of thousands of people packed the narrow stone streets. Rivers of pilgrims flooded the marketplace. Jesus elbowed his way through the sea of people as evening was about to fall. He walked into the temple area, looked around, and walked out.

Want to know what he saw? Then read what he did on Monday, the next morning when he returned. "Jesus went into the Temple and threw out all the people who were buying and selling there. He turned over the tables of those who were exchanging different kinds of money, and he upset the benches of those who were selling doves. Jesus said to all the people there, 'It is written in the Scriptures, "My Temple will be called a house for prayer." But you are changing it into a "hideout for robbers." ' "[3]

What did he see? Hucksters. Faith peddlers. What lit the fire under Jesus' broiler? What was his first thought on Monday? People in the temple making a franchise out of the faith.

It was Passover week. The Passover was the highlight of the Jewish calendar. People came from all regions and many countries to be present for the celebration. Upon arriving they were obligated to meet two requirements.

"My Temple will be called a house for prayer. But you are changing it into a 'hideout for robbers.'"

MATTHEW 21:13

First, an animal sacrifice, usually a dove. The dove had to be perfect, without blemish. The animal could be brought in from any-where, but odds were that if you brought a sacrifice from another place, yours would be considered insufficient by the authorities in the temple. So, under the guise of keeping the sacrifice pure, the dove sellers sold doves—at their price.

Second, the people had to pay a tax, a temple tax. It was due every year. During Passover the tax had to be rendered in local currency. Knowing many foreigners would be in Jerusalem to pay the tax, money changers conveniently set up tables and offered to exchange the foreign money for local—for a modest fee, of course.

It's not difficult to see what angered Jesus. Pilgrims journeyed days to see God, to witness the holy, to worship His Majesty. But before they were taken into the presence of God, they were taken to the cleaners. What was promised and what was delivered were two different things.

Want to anger God? Get in the way of people who want to see him. Want to feel his fury? Exploit people in the name of God.

Mark it down. Religious hucksters poke the fire of divine wrath.

"I've had enough," was written all over the Messiah's face. In he stormed. Doves flapped and tables flew. People scampered and traders scattered.

This was not an impulsive show. This was not a temper tantrum. It was a deliberate act with an intentional message. Jesus had seen the money changers the day before. He went to sleep with pictures of this midway and its barkers in his memory. And when he woke up the next morning, knowing his days were drawing to a close, he chose to make a point: "You cash in on my people and you've got me to answer to." God will never hold guiltless those who exploit the privilege of worship.

Mark it down and beware: there are hucksters in God's house. Don't be fooled by their looks. Don't be dazzled by their words. Be careful. Remember why Jesus purged the temple. Those closest to it may be the farthest from it.

COURAGE TO DREAM AGAIN

Eighty-year-old shepherds don't usually play chicken with Pharaohs . . . but don't tell that to Moses.

Teenage shepherds don't normally have showdowns with giants . . . but don't tell that to David.

Night-shift shepherds don't usually get to hear angels sing and see God in a stable . . . but don't tell that to the Bethlehem bunch.

And for sure don't tell that to God. He's made an eternity out of making the earthbound airborne. And he gets angry when people's wings are clipped. Such is the message of the fig tree drama, a peculiar scene involving a fruitless fig tree and a mountain in the ocean.

Jesus and his disciples walked to Jerusalem on Monday morning after spending the night in Bethany. He was hungry and saw a fig tree on the side of the road. As he approached the tree, he noticed that though it had leaves, it had no fruit. Something about a tree with no fruit reminded him of what he saw in the temple on Sunday and what he is going to do in the temple later that day.[1]

So he denounced the tree. "You will never again have fruit." The tree immediately dried up.

"If you have faith, it will happen."

MATTHEW 21:21

The next day, Tuesday, the disciples see what has happened to the tree. They are amazed. Just twenty-four hours before, the tree had been green and healthy; now it is barren and dry.

"How did the fig tree dry up so quickly?" they ask.

Jesus gives them this answer, "I tell you the truth, if you have faith and do not doubt, you will be able to do what I did to this tree and even more. You will be able to say to this mountain, 'Go, fall into the sea.' And if you have faith, it will happen. If you believe, you will get anything you ask for in prayer."[2]

What's the point? God can't stomach lukewarm faith. He is angered by a religion that puts on a show but ignores the service—and that is precisely the religion he was facing during his last week. And the religion he had faced his entire ministry.

When he served they complained.

They complained that his disciples ate on the wrong day. They complained that he healed on the wrong day. They complained that he forgave the wrong people. They complained that he hung out with the wrong crowd and had the wrong influence on the children. But, still worse, every time he tried to set people free, the religious leaders attempted to tie them down. Those closest to the temple were quickest with the shackles.

The message of the fig tree is not for all of us to have the same fruit. The message is for us to have some fruit. Not easy. Jesus knows that. "If you have faith and do not doubt, you will be able to do what I did to this tree and even more."

Faith in whom? Religion? Hardly. Religion is the hoax Jesus is out to disclose. In fact, when Jesus said, "You will be able to say to this mountain, 'Go, fall into the sea,' " he was probably looking up from the Kidron Valley to the Temple Mount—the temple known to many as Mount Zion. If that is the case, you have reason to smile as Jesus tells you what to do with the church that tries to cage your flight, "Tell it to jump into the lake."

No, the faith is not in religion, the faith is in God. A hardy, daring faith which believes God will do what is right, every time. And that God will do what it takes—whatever it takes—to bring his children home.

He is the shepherd in search of his lamb. His legs are scratched, his feet are sore and his eyes are burning. He scales the cliffs and traverses the fields. He explores the caves. He cups his hands to his mouth and calls into the canyon.

And the name he calls is yours.

He wants you home.

It is only in light of such passion that we can understand this incredible promise: "If you believe, you will get anything you ask for in prayer."[3]

Don't reduce this grand statement to the category of new cars and pay-checks. Don't limit the promise of this passage to the selfish pool of perks and favors. The fruit God assures is far greater than earthly wealth. His dreams are much greater than promotions and proposals.

God wants you to fly. He wants you to fly free of yesterday's guilt. He wants you to fly free of today's fears. He wants you to fly free of tomorrow's grave. Sin, fear, and death. These are the mountains he has moved. These are the prayers he will answer. That is the fruit he will grant. This is what he longs to do: he longs to set you free so you can fly . . . fly home.

Tuesday

OF CALLUSES
AND COMPASSION

*P*eculiar, this childhood church memory of mine.

For many, early church recollections are made of zippered Bibles, patent leather Easter shoes, Christmas pageants, or Sunday schools. Mine is not so religious. Mine is comprised of calluses, straight pins, and dull sermons.

There I sit, all six years of me, flat-topped and freckled. My father's hand in my lap. It is there to keep me from squirming. A robust preacher is behind the pulpit, one of God's kindest but most monotonous servants. Bored, I turn my attention to my father's hand.

If you didn't know he was a mechanic, one look at his hands would tell you as much. Thick, strong, scrubbed clean but still bearing traces of last week's grease.

I'm intrigued as I run my fingers over the calluses. They rise on the palm like a ridge of hills. Calluses. Layer upon layer of nerveless skin. The hand's defense against hours of squeezing wrenches and twisting screwdrivers.

On the back of the pew in front of me is a collection of attendance cards. At the top of each card is a red ribbon for the visitors to wear. The ribbon is attached to the card by a straight pin.

I have an idea. *I wonder how thick those calluses are? . . .*

I take the pin, and with the skill of a surgeon I begin the insertion. (I told you it was peculiar.) I look up at Dad. He doesn't move. I go deeper. No response. Another eighth of an inch. No flinch. While the rest of the church is intent on the words of a preacher, I'm fascinated by the depth of a callus. I decide to give it a final shove.

"Umph," he grunts, yanking his hand away, closing his fist which only pushes the pin further. His glares at me, my mother turns, and my brother giggles. Something tells me that the same hand will be used later that Sunday to make another point.

Peculiar, this childhood memory. But, even more peculiar is that three decades later, I find myself doing the same thing I did at age six: in church, trying to penetrate calluses with a point. Only now I'm in the pulpit, not the pew. And my tool is truth, not a pin. And the calluses are not on the hand, but on the heart.

Thick, dead skin wrapped around the nerves of the soul. The result of hours of rubbing against the truth without receiving it. Toughened, crusty, lifeless tissue which defies feeling and ignores touch.

The calloused heart.

To such hearts Jesus spoke on his last Tuesday. With the persistence of a man with one final message, his point was intended to prick the soul.

"The kingdom of God will be taken away from you and given to people who do the things God wants in his kingdom."

MATTHEW 21:43

He told two stories which contain a common thread, crimson with guilt: the proclivity of people to reject God's invitation not once or twice, but time and time again.

The first story was that of the landowner.[1] He leased a vineyard to some sharecroppers and, at harvest, sent his servants to collect his share of the grapes. "But the farmers grabbed the servants, beat one, killed another, and then killed a third servant with stones."

The second is the story of the king who prepared a wedding feast for his son.² "When the feast was ready, the king sent his servants to tell the people, but they refused to come."

A landowner whose servants are beaten and killed? A king whose messengers are ignored? Surely the landowner and the king will wash their hands of these people. No doubt they will send the police and the military next.

Wrong.

In both cases they send more emissaries. "So the [landowner] sent some other servants to the farmers, even more than he sent the first time. But the farmers did the same thing to the servants that they had done before."

"Then the king sent other servants, saying, 'Tell those who have been invited that my feast is ready.' "

What surprising tolerance! What unexpected patience! Servant after servant. Messenger after messenger. Jesus verbally painting the picture of a determined God.

God's love is not normal love. It's not normal to love a murderer and adulterer, but God did when he loved David. It isn't normal to love a man who takes his eyes off you, but such was God's love for Solomon.³ It isn't normal to love people who love stone idols more than they love you, but God did when he refused to give up on Israel.

And it was this love that Jesus was describing on his last Tuesday. The same love which, on Friday, would take him to the cross.

The cross, the zenith of history. All of the past pointed to it and all of the future would depend upon it. It's the great triumph of heaven: God is on the earth. And it is the great tragedy of earth: man has rejected God.

The religious leaders knew Jesus was speaking about them. Just as their fathers had rejected the prophets, now they were rejecting the Prophet—God himself.

Jesus spoke to those who had turned their backs on history. He spoke to those who had blatantly ignored sign after sign, servant after servant. It wasn't as if they had just skipped a paragraph or missed a punchline. It wasn't as if they had misunderstood a chapter. They had missed the whole book. God had come into their city, walked down their street, knocked on their door, and they refused to let him in.

For that reason—because they had refused to believe—Jesus speaks the most sobering words in the Gospel of Matthew: "The kingdom of God will be taken away from you and given to people who do the things God wants in his kingdom."[4]

God is intolerant of the calloused heart.

He is patient with our mistakes. He is longsuffering with our stumbles. He doesn't get angry at our questions. He doesn't turn away when we struggle. But when we repeatedly reject his message, when we are insensitive to his pleadings, when he changes history itself to get our attention and we still don't listen, he honors our request.

"You refuse to listen," Paul said to the Jews. "You are judging yourselves not worthy of having eternal life! So we will now go to the people of other nations."[5]

Note it was not God who made the people unworthy. It was their refusal to listen that excluded them from grace. Jesus condemns the cold heart, the soul so overgrown with self and selfishness that it would blaspheme the source of hope, the heart so evil that it would see the Prince of Peace and call him the Lord of the Flies.[6]

Fifty-five

Such blasphemy is unforgivable, not because of God's unwillingness to forgive, but man's unwillingness to seek forgiveness. The calloused heart is the cursed heart. The calloused heart represents the eyes that won't see the obvious and the ears that won't hear the plain. As a result, they do not seek God and pardon will not be given because pardon will not be sought.

Perhaps my childhood memory is not so peculiar after all. In a way it is the story of the gospel: Jesus piercing his hands in order to prick our hearts.

CHAPTER TEN

YOU'RE INVITED

God is an inviting God. He invited Mary to birth his son, the disciples to fish for men, the adulteress to start over, and Thomas to touch his wounds. God is the King who prepares the palace, sets the table, and invites his subjects to come in.

In fact, it seems his favorite word is *come.*

"*Come,* let us talk about these things. Though your sins are like scarlet, they can be as white as snow."[1]

"All you who are thirsty, *come* and drink."[2]

"*Come* to me, all of you who are tired and have heavy loads, and I will give you rest."[3]

"*Come* to the wedding feast."[4]

"*Come* follow me, and I will make you fish for people."[5]

"Let anyone who is thirsty *come* to me and drink."[6]

God is a God who invites. God is a God who calls. God is a God who opens the door and waves his hand pointing pilgrims to a full table.

"Come to the wedding feast."

MATTHEW 22:4

His invitation is not just for a meal, however, it is for life. An invitation to come into his kingdom and take up residence in a tearless, graveless, painless world. Who can come? Whoever wishes. The invitation is at once universal and personal.

In the last week of his life, Jesus offered two stories about urgent invitations.

The first is about two sons whose father invites them to work in the vineyard.[7] Their invitations are identical; their responses opposite. One says no, then changes his mind and goes. The other says yes, then changes his mind and stays.

The second story is about a king who prepares a wedding feast for his son.[8] He invites the people to come, but they don't. Some ignore the invitation, some give excuses about being too busy, others actually kill the servants bearing the invitation.

Have you ever wondered how Jesus felt as he told these stories? If you've ever had a personal invitation ignored, you know how he felt. Most people don't reject Jesus . . . they just don't give his invitation serious thought.

Oh, that would hurt. You see, it's one thing to be rejected. It's another not to be taken seriously. Nothing stabs deeper than to give a once-in-a-million, for-your-eyes-only invitation and have it relegated to a list of decisions to be made next week.

Jesus gives the invitation. "Here I am! I stand at the door and knock."[9] To know God is to receive his invitation. Not just to hear it, not just to study it, not just to acknowledge it, but to receive it. It is possible to learn much about God's invitation and never respond to it personally.

Yet his invitation is clear and non-negotiable. He gives all and we give him all. Simple and absolute. He is clear in what he asks and clear in what he offers. The choice is up to us.

Isn't it incredible that God leaves the choice to us? Think about it. There are many things in life we can't choose. We can't, for example, choose the weather. We can't control the economy.

We can't choose whether or not we are born with a big nose or blue eyes or a lot of hair. We can't even choose how people respond to us.

But we can choose where we spend eternity. The big choice, God leaves to us. The critical decision is ours.

What are you doing with God's invitation?

What are you doing with his personal request that you live with him forever?

That is the only decision which really matters. Whether or not you take the job transfer is not critical. Whether or not you buy a new car is not crucial. What college you choose or what profession you select is important, but not compared to where you spend eternity. That is the decision you will remember.

What are you doing with his invitation?

I write as I wait in a large room of our county courthouse. I am here by invitation. As I look around me, I see a hundred or so strangers who also received the same jury summons. They read magazines. They flip through newspapers. They stand and stretch. They do office work. And I ponder the irony of finishing a chapter on God's invitation in a room where I wait for the judge to call my name.

Every few minutes the muffled conversations are silenced by an official-looking gentleman who will enter the room and call names: Yvonne Campbell, Johnny Solis, Thomas Adams. Those he calls will be given instructions and the rest of us return to our activities.

I'm apprehensive about the interview: I don't know what the judge will do. I don't know what the judge will ask. I don't know what the judge will require. I don't know what the outcome will be. I don't even know who the judge is.

So, I'm a bit anxious.

However this isn't my first invitation to appear before a judge. I have another summons, "It is appointed for men to die once, and after that comes judgment."[10] But I don't feel the same anxiety about that appointment.

For I know what the judge will do. I know what the outcome will be. And most of all, I know who the judge is . . . he's my Father.

WHAT MAN
DARED NOT DREAM

We have made many heroes, from King Arthur to Kennedy; Lincoln to Lindbergh; Socrates to Santa to Superman. We give it the best we can, every benefit of every doubt, every supernatural strength, and for a brief shining moment we have the hero we need—the king who can deliver Camelot. But then the truth leaks and fact surfaces amidst the fiction and the chinks in the armor are seen. And we realize that the heroes, as noble as they may have been, as courageous as they were, were conceived in the same stained society as you and I.

"What do you think about the Christ? Whose son is he?"
MATTHEW 22:42

Except one. There was one who claimed to come from a different place. There was one who, though he had the appearance of a man, claimed to have the origin of God. There was one who, while wearing the face of a Jew, had the image of the Creator.

Those who saw him—really saw him—knew there was something different. At his touch blind beggars saw. At his command crippled legs walked. At his embrace empty lives filled with vision.

He fed thousands with one basket. He stilled a storm with one command. He raised the dead with one proclamation. He changed lives with one request. He rerouted the history of the world with one life, lived in one country, was born in one manger, and died on one hill.

During his final week he summarized his claims with one question. Speaking of himself he asked his disciples, "What do you think about the Christ? Whose son is he?"[1]

A probing question. A properly positioned question. The "what" is answered by the "who." What you think about the Christ is embosomed in whose son he is. Note Jesus didn't ask, "What do you think about the Christ and his teachings?" or, "What do you think about the Christ and his opinions on social issues?" or, "What do you think about the Christ and his ability to lead people?"

After three years of ministry, hundreds of miles, thousands of miracles, innumerable teachings, Jesus asks, "Who?" Jesus bids the people to ponder not what he has done but who he is.

It's the ultimate question of the Christ: Whose son is he?

Is he the son of God or the sum of our dreams? Is he the force of creation or a figment of our imagination?

When we ask that question about Santa, the answer is the culmination of our desires. A depiction of our fondest dreams.

Not so when we ask it about Jesus. For no one could ever dream a person as incredible as he is. The idea that a virgin would be selected by God to bear himself. . . . The notion that God would don a scalp and toes and two eyes. . . . The thought that the King of the universe would sneeze and burp and get bit by mosquitoes. . . . It's too incredible. Too revolutionary. We would never create such a Savior. We aren't that daring.

When we create a redeemer, we keep him safely distant in his faraway castle. We allow him only the briefest of encounters with us. We permit him to swoop in and out with his sleigh before we can draw too near. We wouldn't ask him to take up residence in the midst of a contaminated people. In our wildest imaginings we wouldn't conjure a king who becomes one of us.

But God did. God did what we wouldn't dare dream. He did what we couldn't imagine. He became a man so we could trust him. He became a sacrifice so we could know him. And he defeated death so we could follow him.

It defies logic. It is a divine insanity. A holy incredibility. Only a God beyond systems and common sense could create a plan as absurd as this. Yet, it is the very impossibility of it all that makes it possible. The wildness of the story is its strongest witness.

For only a God could create a plan this mad. Only a Creator beyond the fence of logic could offer such a gift of love.

What man can't do, God does.

When it comes to eternity, forgiveness, purpose, and truth, go to the manger. Kneel with the shepherds. Worship the God who dared to do what man dared not dream.

CHAPTER TWELVE

UNCLUTTERED FAITH

edtime is a bad time for kids. No child understands the logic of going to bed while there is energy left in the body or hours left in the day.

My children are no exception. A few nights ago, after many objections and countless groans, the girls were finally in their gowns, in their beds, and on their pillows. I slipped into the room to give them a final kiss. Andrea, the five-year-old was still awake, just barely, but awake. After I kissed her, she lifted her eyelids one final time and said, "I can't wait until I wake up."

Oh, for the attitude of a five-year-old! That simple uncluttered passion for living that can't wait for tomorrow. A philosophy of life that reads, "Play hard, laugh hard, and leave the worries to your father." A bottomless well of optimism flooded by a perpetual spring of faith. Is it any wonder Jesus said we must have the heart of a child before we can enter the kingdom of heaven?

Perhaps you long to wake up to the same life my daughter does: playful, peaceful, and secure. You haven't found it in the world and you've peeked in the church doors and aren't too sure about what you see there either.

Or maybe you've done more than peek through the church doors, you've gone in and gotten to work. You've baked, visited, volunteered, and taught. But instead of rest you got stress. And now you are puzzled because

Jesus said you should feel at peace and since you don't, it certainly must be your fault. God wouldn't say that and not do it, would he? So in addition to being confused by the world and the church you are confused at your own inability to make sense out of it all.

Whew! Being a Christian is hard work!

It's not supposed to be though. Complicated religion wasn't made by God. Reading Matthew 23 will convince you of that. It is the crackdown of Christ on midway religion.

If you've always thought of Jesus as a pale-faced, milquetoast Tiny Tim, then read this chapter and see the other side: an angry father denouncing the pimps who have prostituted his children.

Six times he calls them hypocrites. Five times he calls them blind. Seven times he denounces them and once he prophesies their ruin. Not what you would call a public relations presentation.

But in the midst of the roaring river of words there is a safe island of instruction. Somewhere between bursts of fire Jesus holsters his pistol, turns to the wide-eyed disciples, and describes the essence of simple faith. Four verses: a reading as brief as it is practical. Call it Christ's solution to complicated Christianity.

"So do not let anyone make rules for you."

Colossians 2:16

"You must not be called 'Teacher,' because you have only one Teacher, and you are all brothers and sisters together. And don't call any person on earth 'Father,' because you have one Father, who is in heaven. And you should not be called 'Master,' because you have only one Master, the Christ. Whoever is your servant is the greatest among you. Whoever makes himself great will be made humble. Whoever makes himself humble will be made great."[1]

How do you simplify your faith? How do you get rid of the clutter? How do you discover a joy worth waking up to? Simple. Get rid of the middleman.

Discover truth for yourself. "You have only one Teacher, and you are all brothers and sisters together."[2]

Develop trust for yourself. "Don't call any person on earth 'Father,' because you have one Father, who is in heaven."[3]

Discern his will for yourself. "You have only one Master, the Christ."[4]

There are some who position themselves between you and God. There are some who suggest the only way to get to God is through them. There is the great teacher who has the final word on Bible teaching. There is the father who must bless your acts. There is the spiritual master who will tell you what God wants you to do. Jesus' message for complicated religion is to remove these middlemen.

He's not saying that you don't need teachers, elders, or counselors. He is saying, however, that we are all brothers and sisters and have equal access to the Father. Simplify your faith by seeking God for yourself. No confusing ceremonies necessary. No mysterious rituals required. No elaborate channels of command or levels of access.

You have a Bible? You can study. You have a heart? You can pray. You have a mind? You can think.

Seek the simple faith. Major in the majors. Focus on the critical. Long for God.

"I can't wait to wake up," are the words of a child's faith. The reason Andrea can say them is because her world is simple. She plays hard, she laughs much, and she leaves the worries to her father.

Let's do the same.

CHAPTER THIRTEEN

SURVIVING LIFE

*S*ome years ago we took a family vacation to Santa Fe, New Mexico. Denalyn and I decided to be adventurous and ride the rapids of the Rio Grande. We drove to the designated spot and there met the guide and the other courageous tourists.

His instructions were foreboding.

"When you fall in the water . . ." he began.

"And when you find yourself floating in the river . . ."

"And when the boat flips over . . ." I was beginning to get nervous. I elbowed Denalyn and whispered, "Notice he doesn't say 'if'."

Nor did Jesus. Jesus didn't say, "In this world you may have trouble" or, "In this world there are some who have trouble." No, he assured us, "In this world you will have trouble."[1] If you have a pulse you will have pain. If you are a person you will have problems.

In Matthew 24 Jesus prepares his disciples by telling them what will happen.

"Many will come in my name, saying, 'I am the Christ,' and they will fool many people."[2]

"You will hear about wars and stories of wars that are coming, but don't

> *"But those people who keep their faith until the end will be saved. The Good News about God's kingdom will be preached in all the world, to every nation. Then the end will come."*
>
> MATTHEW 24:13-14

be afraid. These things must happen before the end comes."[3]

"There will be times when there is no food for people to eat, and there will be earthquakes in different places. These things are like the first pains when something new is about to be born."[4]

"Then people will arrest you, hand you over to be hurt, and kill you. They will hate you because you believe in me."[5]

Far from a pep rally don't you think? More like a last word given by an officer before the soldiers go to battle. More like a lesson Charles Hall would give his demolition team.

Charles Hall blows up bombs for a living. He is a part of the EOD — the Explosive Ordinance Demolition. He is paid $1,500 a week to walk the sands of post-war Kuwait searching for live mines or discarded grenades.

Richard Lowther, another EOD expert, has spent years blowing up some of the thousands of sea mines left over from World Wars I and II. He said, "Every time I pick up the paper and read about a new civil war I think 'Great, as soon as it's over I'll be there.'"[6]

You and I and these EODs have a lot in common: treacherous trails through explosive territories. Problems which lay partly obscured by the sand. A constant threat of losing life or limb.

And most significant, we, like the demolition team, are called to walk through a mine field which we didn't create. Such is the case with many of life's struggles. We didn't create them, but we have to live with them.

Jesus is honest about the life we are called to lead. There is no guarantee that just because we belong to him we will go unscathed. No promise is found in Scripture that says when you follow the king you are exempt from battle. No, often just the opposite is the case.

How do we survive the battle? How do we endure the fray?

Jesus gives three certainties. Three assurances. Three absolutes. Imagine him leaning closer and looking deeply into the wide eyes of the disciples. Knowing the jungle they are about to enter, he gives them three compasses which, if used, will keep them on the right trail.

First, assurance of victory: "Those people who keep their faith until the end will be saved."[7]

He doesn't say if you succeed you will be saved. Or if you come out on top you will be saved. He says if you endure. An accurate rendering would be, "If you hang in there until the end . . . if you go the distance."

The Brazilians have a great phrase for this. In Portuguese, a person who has the ability to hang in and not give up has *garra*. *Garra* means "claws." What imagery! A person with *garra* has claws which burrow into the side of the cliff and keep him from falling.

So do the saved. They may get close to the edge, they may even stumble and slide. But they will dig their nails into the rock of God and hang on.

Secondly, Jesus gives the assurance of accomplishment: "The Good News about God's kingdom will be preached in all the world, to every nation."[8]

In 1066 one of the most decisive battles in the history of the world was fought. William, Duke of Normandy, dared to invade England. The English were a formidable opponent anywhere, but next to invincible in their own land.

But William had something the English did not. He had invented a device which gave his army a heavy advantage in battle. He had an edge: the stirrup.

Conventional wisdom of the day was that a horse was too unstable a platform from which to fight. As a result soldiers would ride their horses to the battlefield and then dismount before engaging in combat. But the Norman army, standing secure in their stirrups, were able to ride down the English. They were faster and they were stronger.

The stirrup led to the conquest of England. Without it, William might never have challenged such an enemy. And this book might have been written in Old English.

Because they had a way to stand in the battle, they were victorious after the battle. Jesus' assurance of victory was daring. Look at his listeners: upcountry fishermen and laborers whose eyes bug at the sight of a big city. You'd have been hard-pressed to find anyone who would wage that the prophecy would come to pass.

But it did, just fifty-three days later. Fifty-three days later Jews were in Jerusalem from "every country in the world."[9] Peter stood before them and told them about Jesus.

The disciples were emboldened with the assurance that the task would be completed. Because they had a way to stand in the battle, they were victorious after the battle. They had an edge . . . and so do we.

Lastly, Jesus gives us assurance of completion: "Then the end will come."[10]

An intriguing verse is found in 1 Thessalonians 4:16, "The Lord himself will come down from heaven with a loud command."

Have you ever wondered what that command will be? It will be the inaugural word of heaven. It will be the first audible message most have heard from God. It will be the word which closes one age and opens a new one.

I think I know what the command will be. I could very well be wrong, but I think the command which puts an end to the pains of the earth and initiates the joys of heaven will be two words:

"No more."

Seventy

The King of kings will raise his pierced hand and proclaim, "No more."

The angels will stand and the Father will speak, "No more."

Every person who lives and who ever lived will turn toward the sky and hear God announce, "No more."

No more loneliness.

No more tears.

No more death. No more sadness. No more crying. No more pain.

As John sat on the Island of Patmos surrounded by sea and separated from friends he dreamt of the day when God would say, "No more."

This same disciple who had heard Jesus speak these words of assurance over a half a century before now knew what they meant. I wonder if he could hear the voice of Jesus in his memory.

"The end will come."

For those who live for this world, that's bad news. But for those who live for the world to come, it's an encouraging promise.

You're in a mine field, my friend, and it's only a matter of time: "For in this world you will have trouble. . . ." Next time you are tossed into a river as you ride the rapids of life, remember his words of assurance.

Those who endure will be saved.

The gospel will be preached.

The end will come.

You can count on it.

CHAPTER FOURTEEN

SANDCASTLE STORIES

Hot sun. Salty air. Rhythmic waves.

A little boy is on the beach. On his knees he scoops and packs the sand with plastic shovels into a bright red bucket. Then he upends the bucket on the surface and lifts it. And, to the delight of the little architect, a castle tower is created.

All afternoon he will work. Spooning out the moat. Packing the walls. Bottle tops will be sentries. Popsicle sticks will be bridges. A sandcastle will be built.

Big city. Busy streets. Rumbling traffic.

A man is in his office. At his desk he shuffles papers into stacks and delegates assignments. He cradles the phone on his shoulder and punches the keyboard with his fingers. Numbers are juggled and contracts are signed and much to the delight of the man, a profit is made.

All his life he will work. Formulating the plans. Forecasting the future. Annuities will be sentries. Capital gains will be bridges. An empire will be built.

Two builders of two castles. They have much in common. They shape granules into grandeurs. They see nothing and make something. They are diligent and determined. And for both the tide will rise and the end will come.

Yet, that is where the similarities cease. For the boy sees the end while the man ignores it. Watch the boy as the dusk approaches.

As the waves near, the wise child jumps to his feet and begins to clap. There is no sorrow. No fear. No regret. He knew this would happen. He is not surprised. And when the great breaker crashes into his castle and his masterpiece is sucked into the sea, he smiles. He smiles, picks up his tools, takes his father's hand, and goes home.

The grownup, however, is not so wise. As the wave of years collapses on his castle he is terrified. He hovers over the sandy monument to protect it. He blocks the waves from the walls he has made. Salt-water soaked and shivering he snarls at the incoming tide.

"It's my castle," he defies.

The ocean need not respond. Both know to whom the sand belongs.

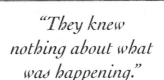

"They knew nothing about what was happening."

MATTHEW 24:39

During the last week of his life, Jesus took valuable time to tell us to learn the lesson of the waves and prepare for the end.

Remember, the reason we are studying the last week of Christ is to see what is on his heart. Hear what he says. See who he touches. Witness what he does. We've seen his compassion for the forgotten. We've seen his contempt for the fake. Now a third passion surfaces—his concern for our readiness. "No one knows when that day or time will be, not the angels in heaven, not even the Son. Only the Father knows."[1]

His message is unmistakable: He will return, but no one knows when. So, be ready.

It's the message of the parable of the virgins.[2]

It's the message of the parable of the talents.[3]

It's the message of the parable of the sheep and the goats.[4]

It's a message we must heed.

But it is a message often ignored.

I was reminded of this not long ago when I boarded a plane. I walked down the aisle, found my seat, and sat next to a strange sight.

The man seated next to me was in a robe and slippers. He was dressed for the living room, not for a journey. His seat was odd, too. Whereas my seat was the cloth type you normally see, his was fine leather.

"Imported," he said, when he noticed I was looking. "Bought it in Argentina and put it on myself."

Before I could speak he pointed to some inlaid stones in the armrest. "The rubies I purchased in Africa. They cost me a fortune."

That was only the beginning. His fold-down table was of mahogany. There was a portable TV installed next to the window. A tiny ceiling fan and globed light hung above us.

I had never seen anything like it.

My question was the obvious one, "Why did you spend so much time and expense on an airline seat?"

"I live here," he explained. "I make my home on the plane."

"You never get off?"

"Never! How could I deboard and leave such comfort?"

Incredible. The man made a home out of a mode of transportation. He made a residence out of a journey. Hard to believe? You think I'm stretching the truth? Well, maybe I haven't seen such foolishness in a plane, but I have in life. And so have you.

You've seen people treat this world like it was a permanent home. It's not. You've seen people pour time and energy into life like it will last forever.

It won't. You've seen people so proud of what they have done, that they hope they will never have to leave—they will.

We all will. We are in transit. Someday the plane will stop and the de-boarding will begin.

Wise are those who are ready when the pilot says to get off.

I don't know much, but I do know how to travel. Carry little. Eat light. Take a nap. And get off when you reach the city.

And I don't know much about sandcastles. But children do. Watch them and learn. Go ahead and build, but build with a child's heart. When the sun sets and the tides take—applaud. Salute the process of life, take your father's hand, and go home.

CHAPTER FIFTEEN

BE READY

It may surprise you that Jesus made preparedness the theme of his last sermon. It did me. I would have preached on love or family or the importance of church. Jesus didn't. Jesus preached on what many today consider to be old-fashioned. He preached on being ready for heaven and staying out of hell.

It's his message when he tells of the wise and the foolish servant.[1] The wise one was ready for the return of the master, the foolish one was not.

It's his message when he tells about the ten bridesmaids. Five were wise and five were foolish.[2] The wise ones were ready when the groom came and the foolish ones were at the corner store looking for more oil.

It's his message when he tells of the three servants and the bags of gold.[3] Two servants put the money to work and made more money for the master. The third hid his in a hole. The first two were ready and rewarded when the master returned. The third was unprepared and punished.

Be ready.

That is the theme of Jesus' last sermon, "So always be ready, because you don't know the day your Lord will come."[4] He didn't tell when the day of the Lord would be, but he did describe what the day would be like. It's a day no one will miss.

Every person who has ever lived will be present at that final gathering.

Every heart that has ever beat. Every mouth that has ever spoken. On that day you will be surrounded by a sea of people. Rich, poor. Famous, unknown. Kings, bums. Brilliant, demented. All will be present. And all will be looking in one direction. All will be looking at him. Every human being.

"The Son of Man will come again in his great glory."[5]

You won't look at anyone else. No side-glances to see what others are wearing. No whispers about new jewelry or comments about who is present. At this, the greatest gathering in history, you will have eyes for only one—the Son of Man. Wrapped in splendor. Shot through with radiance. Imploded with light and magnetic in power.

Jesus describes this day with certainty.

He leaves no room for doubt. He doesn't say he may return, or might return, but that he *will* return. By the way, one-twentieth of your New Testament speaks about his return. There are over three hundred references to his second coming. Twenty-three of the twenty-seven New Testament books speak of it. And they speak of it with confidence.

"So always be ready, because you don't know the day your Lord will come."

MATTHEW 24:42

"You also must be ready, because the Son of Man will come at a time you don't expect him."[6]

". . . Jesus, who has been taken from you into heaven, will come back in the same way you have seen him go into heaven."[7]

". . . he will come a second time, not to offer himself for sin, but to bring salvation to those who are waiting for him."[8]

". . . the day of the Lord will come like a thief in the night."[9]

His return is certain.

His return is final.

Upon his return "he will separate them into two groups as a shepherd separates the sheep from the goats. The Son of Man will put the sheep on his right and the goats on his left."[10]

The word *separate* is a sad word. To separate a mother from a daughter, a father from a son, a husband from a wife. To separate people on earth is sorrowful, but to think of it being done for eternity is horrible.

Especially when one group is destined for heaven and the other group is going to hell.

We don't like to talk about hell, do we? In intellectual circles the topic of hell is regarded as primitive and foolish. It's not logical. "A loving God wouldn't send people to hell." So we dismiss it.

But to dismiss it is to dismiss a core teaching of Jesus. The doctrine of hell is not one developed by Paul, Peter, or John. It is taught by Jesus himself.

And to dismiss it is to dismiss much more. It is to dismiss the presence of a loving God and the privilege of a free choice. Let me explain.

We are free either to love God or not. He invites us to love him. He urges us to love him. He came that we might love him. But, in the end, the choice is yours and mine. To take that choice from each of us, for him to force us to love him, would be less than love.

God explains the benefits, outlines the promises, and articulates very clearly the consequences. And then, in the end, he leaves the choice to us.

Hell was not prepared for people. Hell "was prepared for the devil and his angels."[11] For a person to go to hell, then, is for a person to go against God's intended destiny. "God has not destined us to the terrors of judgment, but to the full attainment of salvation through our Lord Jesus Christ."[12] Hell is man's choice, not God's choice.

Consider, then, this explanation of hell: Hell is the chosen place of the person who loves self more than God, who loves sin more than his Savior, who loves this world more than God's world. Judgment is that moment when God looks at the rebellious and says, "Your choice will be honored."

To reject the dualistic outcome of history and say there is no hell leaves gaping holes in any banner of a just God. To say there is no hell is to say God condones the rebellious, unrepentant heart. To say there is no hell is to portray God with eyes blind to the hunger and evil in the world. To say there is no hell is to say that God doesn't care that people are beaten and massacred, that he doesn't care that women are raped or families wrecked. To say there is no hell is to say God has no justice, no sense of right and wrong, and eventually to say God has no love. For true love hates what is evil.

Hell is the ultimate expression of a just Creator.

The parables of the wise and loyal servant, the wise and foolish brides-maids, and loyal and wicked servants, all point to the same conclusion: "Everyone must die once and be judged."[13] *Eternity is to be taken seriously.* A judgment is coming.

Our task on earth is singular—to choose our eternal home. You can afford many wrong choices in life. You can choose the wrong career and survive, the wrong city and survive, the wrong house and survive. You can even choose the wrong mate and survive. But there is one choice that must be made correctly and that is your eternal destiny.

It's interesting that Jesus' first and last sermons have the same message. In his first sermon, the Sermon on the Mount, Jesus calls you and me to choose between the rock and the sand,[14] the wide gate and the narrow gate, the wide road and the narrow road, the big crowd and the small crowd, the certainty of hell and the joy of heaven.[15] In his last sermon he calls us to do the same. He calls us to be ready.

While on one of his expeditions to the Antarctic, Sir Ernest Shackleton left some of his men on Elephant Island with the intent of returning for them and carrying them back to England. But he was delayed. By the time he could go back for them the sea had frozen and he had no access to the island. Three times he tried to reach them, but was prevented by the ice. Finally, on his fourth try, he broke through and found a narrow channel.

Much to his surprise, he found the crewmen waiting for him, supplies packed and ready to board. They were soon on their way back to England. He asked them how they knew to be ready for him. They told him they didn't know when he would return, but they were sure he would. So every morning, the leader rolled up his bag and packed his gear and told the crew to do the same, saying, "Get your things ready, boys. The boss may come today."[16]

The crew leader did his crew a favor by keeping them prepared.

Jesus has done us a service by urging us to do the same: Be ready.

CHAPTER SIXTEEN

THE SIGN OF THE SAVED

*I*n the last sermon recorded by Matthew, Jesus describes a scene—the last scene, the final judgment. In his final discourse, he puts into words the very message he has put into actions, "Love for the least."

We saw in the last chapter the significance of the final judgment. We saw its certainty—there is no doubt as to Jesus' return. We saw its totality—everyone will be there. And we saw its finality—for on that day Jesus will separate the sheep from the goats, the good from the wicked.

On what basis will he make his selection? The answer may surprise you. "I was hungry, and you gave me food. I was thirsty, and you gave me something to drink. I was alone and away from home, and you invited me into your house. I was without clothes, and you gave me something to wear. I was sick, and you cared for me. I was in prison, and you visited me."[1]

"Anything you did for even the least of my people here, you also did for me."

MATTHEW 25:40

What is the sign of the saved? Their scholarship? Their willingness to go to foreign lands? Their ability to amass an audience and preach? Their skillful pens and hope-filled volumes? Their great miracles? No.

The sign of the saved is their love for the least.

Those put on the right hand of God will be those who gave food to the hungry, drink to the thirsty, warmth to the lonely, clothing to the naked, comfort to the sick, and friendship to the imprisoned.

The sign of the saved is their love for the least.

Did you note how simple the works are? Jesus doesn't say, "I was sick and you healed me. . . . I was in prison and you liberated me. . . . I was lonely and you built a retirement home for me. . . ." He doesn't say, "I was thirsty and you gave me spiritual counsel."

No fanfare. No hoopla. No media coverage. Just good people doing good things.

For when we do good things to others we do good things to God.

When Francis of Asissi turned his back on wealth to seek God in simplicity, he stripped naked and walked out of the city. He soon encountered a leper on the side of the road. He passed him, then stopped and went back and embraced the diseased man. Francis then continued on his journey. After a few steps he turned to look again at the leper, but no one was there.

For the rest of his life, he believed the leper was Jesus Christ. He may have been right.

Jesus lives in the forgotten. He has taken up residence in the ignored. He has made a mansion amidst the ill. If we want to see God we must go among the broken and beaten and there we will see him.

"He rewards those who truly want to find him,"[2] is the promise. "Anything you did for even the least of my people here, you also did for me,"[3] is the plan.

Perhaps you read about the fellow in Philadelphia who went to the flea market and found a frame he liked. It was only a couple of bucks, this dusty print of a country church. It was torn and faded, but the guy liked the frame so he bought it.

When he got home he opened it up and out tumbled a neatly folded sheet of paper. It was the Declaration of Independence. What everyone had thought was a two-dollar painting at a flea market actually contained one of the original one hundred copies of the Declaration of Independence printed on July 4, 1776.[4]

Valuable surprises are discovered in unlikely sources. True in flea markets and true in life. Make an investment in the people the world has cast off—the homeless, the AIDS patient, the orphan, the divorcee—and you may discover the source of your independence.

Jesus' message is stirring: "The way you treat them is the way you treat me."

Of all the teachings during the last week of Christ, this one is for me the most penetrating. I wish he hadn't said what he said. I wish he'd said that the sign of the saved is the books they have written, for I've written several. I wish he'd said the sign of the saved was the numbers of sermons they've preached, for I've preached hundreds. I wish he'd said the sign of the saved was the audiences they've amassed, for I've spoken to thousands.

But he didn't. His words reminded me that the person who sees Christ is the one who sees the hurting person. To see Jesus, go to the convalescent home, sit down beside the elderly woman, and steady her hand as she puts the spoon in her mouth. To see Jesus, go to the community hospital and ask the nurse to take you to see one who has received no visits. To see Jesus, leave your office and go down the hall and talk to the man who is regretting his divorce and missing his children. To see Jesus, go to the inner city and give a sandwich—not a sermon, but a sandwich—to the bag lady who's made a home out of an overpass.

To see Jesus . . . see the unattractive and forgotten.

Thursday

CHAPTER SEVENTEEN

SERVED BY THE BEST

When I was a young boy I was a part of a church corps which took communion to the shut-ins and hospitalized. We visited those who were unable to come to church but still desired to pray and partake of communion.

I must have been ten or eleven years of age when we went to one hospital room that housed an elderly gentleman who was very weak. He was asleep, so we tried to wake him. We couldn't. We shook him, we spoke to him, we tapped him on the shoulder, but we couldn't stir him.

We hated to leave without performing our duty, but we didn't know what to do.

One of the young guys with me observed that even though the man was asleep his mouth was open. Why not? we said. So we prayed over the cracker and stuck a piece on his tongue. Then we prayed over the grape juice and poured it down his mouth.

He never woke up.

Neither do many today. For some, communion is a sleepy hour in which wafers are eaten and juice is drunk and the soul never stirs. It wasn't intended to be as such.

It was intended to be an I-can't-believe-it's-me-pinch-me-I'm-dreaming invitation to sit at God's table and be served by the King himself.

When you read Matthew's account of the Last Supper, one incredible truth surfaces. Jesus is the person behind it all. It was Jesus who selected the place, designated the time, and set the meal in order. "The chosen time is near. I will have the Passover with my followers at your house."[1]

And at the Supper, Jesus is not a guest, but the host. "And [Jesus] gave to the disciples." The subject of the verbs is the message of the event: "he took . . . he blessed . . . he broke . . . he gave. . . ."

And, at the Supper, Jesus is not the served, but the servant. It is Jesus who, during the Supper, put on the garb of a servant and washed the disciples' feet.[2]

Jesus is the most active one at the table. Jesus is not portrayed as the one who reclines and receives, but as the one who stands and gives.

He still does. The Lord's Supper is a gift to you. The Lord's Supper is a sacrament[3] not a sacrifice.[4]

Often, we think of the Supper as a performance, a time when we are on stage and God is the audience. A ceremony in which we do the work and he does the watching. That's not how it was intended. If it was, Jesus would have taken his seat at the table and relaxed.[5]

That's not what he did. He, instead, fulfilled his role as a rabbi by guiding his disciples through the Passover. He fulfilled his role as a servant by washing their feet. And he fulfilled his role as a Savior by granting them forgiveness of sins.

He was in charge. He was on center stage. He was the person behind and in the moment.

And he still is.

It is the Lord's table you sit at. It is the Lord's Supper you eat. Just as Jesus prayed for his disciples, Jesus begs God for us.[6] When you are called

> *"The master will dress himself to serve and tell the servants to sit at the table, and he will serve them."*
>
> LUKE 12:37

to the table, it might be an emissary who gives the letter, but it is Jesus who wrote it.

It is a holy invitation. A sacred sacrament bidding you to leave the chores of life and enter his splendor.

He meets you at the table.

And when the bread is broken, Christ breaks it. When the wine is poured, Christ pours it. And when your burdens are lifted, it is because the King in the apron has drawn near.

Think about that the next time you go to the table.

One last thought.

What happens on earth is just a warm-up for what will happen in heaven.[7] So the next time the messenger calls you to the table, drop what you are doing and go. Be blessed and be fed and, most importantly, be sure you're still eating at his table when he calls us home.

HE CHOSE YOU

*I*t's nearly midnight when they leave the upper room and descend through the streets of the city. They pass the Lower Pool and exit the Fountain Gate and walk out of Jerusalem. The roads are lined with the fires and tents of Passover pilgrims. Most are asleep, heavied with the evening meal. Those still awake think little of the band of men walking the chalky road.

They pass through the valley and ascend the path which will take them to Gethsemane. The road is steep so they stop to rest. Somewhere within the city walls the twelfth apostle darts down a street. His feet have been washed by the man he will betray. His heart has been claimed by the Evil One he has heard. He runs to find Caiaphas.

The final encounter of the battle has begun.

As Jesus looks at the city of Jerusalem, he sees what the disciples can't. It is here, on the outskirts of Jerusalem, that the battle will end. He sees the staging of Satan. He sees the dashing of the demons. He sees the Evil One preparing for the final encounter. The enemy lurks as a spectre over the hour. Satan, the host of hatred, has seized the heart of Judas and whispered in the ear of Caiaphas. Satan, the master of death, has opened the caverns and prepared to receive the source of light.

"I pray for these followers, but I am also praying for all those who will believe in me because of their teaching."

JOHN 17:20

Hell is breaking loose.

History records it as a battle of the Jews against Jesus. It wasn't. It was a battle of God against Satan.

And Jesus knew it. He knew that before the war was over, he would be taken captive. He knew that before victory would come defeat. He knew that before the throne would come the cup. He knew that before the light of Sunday would come the blackness of Friday.

And he is afraid.

He turns and begins the final ascent to the garden. When he reaches the entry he stops and turns his eyes toward his circle of friends. It will be the last time he sees them before they abandon him. He knows what they will do when the soldiers come. He knows their betrayal is only minutes away.

But he doesn't accuse. He doesn't lecture. Instead, he prays. His last moments with his disciples are in prayer. And the words he speaks are as eternal as the stars which hear them.

Imagine, for a moment, yourself in this situation. Your final hour with a son about to be sent overseas. Your last moments with your dying spouse. One last visit with your parent. What do you say? What do you do? What words do you choose?

It's worth noting that Jesus chose prayer. He chose to pray for us. "I pray for these men. But I am also praying for all people who will believe in me because of the teaching of these men. Father, I pray that all people who believe in me can be one. . . . I pray that these people can also be one in us, so that the world will believe that you sent me."[1]

You need to note that in this final prayer, Jesus prayed for you. You need to underline in red and highlight in yellow his love: "I am also praying for all people who will believe in me because of the teaching." That is you.

As Jesus stepped into the garden, you were in his prayers. As Jesus looked into heaven, you were in his vision. As Jesus dreamed of the day when we will be where he is, he saw you there.

His final prayer was about you. His final pain was for you. His final passion was you.

He then turns, steps into the garden, and invites Peter, James, and John to come. He tells them his soul is "overwhelmed with sorrow to the point of death," and begins to pray.

Never has he felt so alone. What must be done, only he can do. An angel can't do it. No angel has the power to break open hell's gates. A man can't do it. No man has the purity to destroy sin's claim. No force on earth can face the force of evil and win—except God.

"The spirit is willing, but the flesh is weak," Jesus confesses.

His humanity begged to be delivered from what his divinity could see. Jesus, the carpenter, implores. Jesus, the man, peers into the dark pit and begs, "Can't there be another way?"

Did he know the answer before he asked the question? Did his human heart hope his heavenly father had found another way? We don't know. But we do know he asked to get out. We do know he begged for an exit. We do know there was a time when if he could have, he would have turned his back on the whole mess and gone away.

But he couldn't.

He couldn't because he saw you. Right there in the middle of a world which isn't fair. He saw you cast into a river of life you didn't request. He saw you betrayed by those you love. He saw you with a body which gets sick and a heart which grows weak.

He saw you in your own garden of gnarled trees and sleeping friends.

He saw you staring into the pit of your own failures and the mouth of your own grave.

He saw you in your Garden of Gethsemane—and he didn't want you to be alone.

He wanted you to know that he has been there, too. He knows what it's like to be plotted against. He knows what it's like to be confused. He knows what it's like to be torn between two desires. He knows what it's like to smell the stench of Satan. And, perhaps most of all, he knows what it's like to beg God to change his mind and to hear God say so gently, but firmly, "No."

For that is what God says to Jesus. And Jesus accepts the answer. At some moment during that midnight hour an angel of mercy comes over the weary body of the man in the garden. As he stands, the anguish is gone from his eyes. His fist will clench no more. His heart will fight no more.

The battle is won. You may have thought it was won on Golgotha. It wasn't. You may have thought the sign of victory is the empty tomb. It isn't. The final battle was won in Gethsemane. And the sign of conquest is Jesus at peace in the olive trees.

For it was in the garden that he made his decision. He would rather go to hell for you than go to heaven without you.

Friday

CHAPTER NINETEEN

WHEN YOUR WORLD TURNS AGAINST YOU

et up, we must go. Here comes the man who has turned against me."[1]

The words were spoken to Judas. But they could have been spoken to anyone. They could have been spoken to John, to Peter, to James. They could have been spoken to Thomas, to Andrew, to Nathanael. They could have been spoken to the Roman soldiers, to the Jewish leaders. They could have been spoken to Pilate, to Herod, to Caiaphas. They could have been spoken to every person who praised him last Sunday but abandoned him tonight.

Everyone turned against Jesus.

Though the kiss was planted by Judas, the betrayal was committed by all. Every person took a step, but no one took a stand. As Jesus left the garden he walked alone. The world had turned against him. He was betrayed.

Betray. The word is an eighth of an inch above *betroth* in the dictionary, but a world from *betroth* in life. It's a weapon found only in the hands of one you love. Your enemy has no such tool, for only a friend can betray. Betrayal is mutiny. It's a violation of a trust, an inside job.

Would that it were a stranger. Would that it were a random attack. Would that you were a victim of circumstances. But you aren't. You are a victim of a friend.

A sandpaper kiss is placed on your cheek. A promise is made with fingers crossed. You look to your friends and your friends don't look back. You look to the system for justice—the system looks to you as a scapegoat.

You are betrayed. Bitten with a snake's kiss.

It's more than rejection. Rejection opens a wound, betrayal pours the salt.

It's more than loneliness. Loneliness leaves you in the cold, betrayal closes the door.

It's more than mockery. Mockery plunges the knife, betrayal twists it.

It's more than an insult. An insult attacks your pride, betrayal breaks your heart.

Betrayal . . . when your world turns against you.

Betrayal . . . where there is opportunity for love, there is opportunity for hurt.

"In the future you will see the Son of Man sitting at the right hand of God."

MATTHEW 26:64

When betrayal comes, what do you do? Get out? Get angry? Get even? You have to deal with it some way. Let's see how Jesus dealt with it.

Begin by noticing how Jesus saw Judas. "Jesus answered, 'Friend, do what you came to do.' "[2]

Of all the names I would have chosen for Judas it would not have been "friend." What Judas did to Jesus was grossly unfair. There is no indication that Jesus ever mistreated Judas. There is no clue that Judas was ever left out or neglected. When, during the Last Supper, Jesus told the disciples that his betrayer sat at the table, they didn't turn to one another and whisper, "It's Judas. Jesus told us he would do this."

They didn't whisper it because Jesus never said it. He had known it. He had known what Judas would do, but he treated the betrayer as if he were faithful.

It's even more unfair when you consider the betrayal was Judas's idea. The religious leaders didn't seek him, Judas sought them. "What will you pay me for giving Jesus to you?" he asked.[3] The betrayal would have been more palatable had Judas been propositioned by the leaders, but he wasn't. He propositioned them.

And Judas's method . . . again, why did it have to be a kiss?[4]

And why did he have to call him "Teacher"?[5] That's a title of respect. The incongruity of his words, deeds, and actions—I wouldn't have called Judas "friend."

But that is exactly what Jesus called him. Why? Jesus could see something we can't. Let me explain.

Jesus knew Judas had been seduced by a powerful foe. He was aware of the wiles of Satan's whispers (he had just heard them himself). He knew how hard it was for Judas to do what was right.

He didn't justify what Judas did. He didn't minimize the deed. Nor did he release Judas from his choice. But he did look eye to eye with his betrayer and try to understand.

As long as you hate your enemy, a jail door is closed and a prisoner is taken. But when you try to understand and release your foe from your hatred, then the prisoner is released and that prisoner is you.

Perhaps you don't like that idea. Perhaps the thought of forgiveness is unrealistic. Perhaps the idea of trying to understand the Judases in our world is simply too gracious.

My response to you then is a question. What do you suggest? Will harboring the anger solve the problem? Will getting even remove the hurt? Does hatred do any good? Again, I'm not minimizing your hurt or justifying their actions. But I am saying that justice won't come this side of eternity. And demanding that your enemy get his or her share of pain will, in the process, be most painful to you.

May I gently but firmly remind you of something you know but may have forgotten? Life is not fair.

That's not pessimism, it's fact. That's not a complaint, it's just the way things are. I don't like it. Neither do you. We want life to be fair. Ever since the kid down the block got a bike and we didn't, we've been saying the same thing, "That's not fair."

But at some point someone needs to say to us, "Who ever told you life was going to be fair?"

God didn't. He didn't say, "*If* you have many kinds of troubles." He said, "*When* you have many kinds of troubles."[6] Troubles are part of the package. Betrayals are part of our troubles. Don't be surprised when betrayals come. Don't look for fairness here—look instead where Jesus looked.

Jesus looked to the future. Read his words: "In the future you will see the Son of Man coming." While going through hell, Jesus kept his eyes on heaven. While surrounded by enemies, he kept his mind on his father. While abandoned on earth, he kept his heart on home. "In the future you will see the Son of Man sitting at the right hand of God, the Powerful One, and coming on clouds in the sky."[7]

Jesus took a long look into the homeland. Long enough to count his friends. "I could ask my Father and he would give me twelve armies of angels." And seeing them up there gave him strength down here.

By the way, his friends are your friends. The Father's loyalty to Jesus is the Father's loyalty to you. When you feel betrayed, remember that. When you see the torches and feel the betrayer's kiss, remember his words: "I will never leave you; I will never forget you."[8]

Think of home.

YOUR CHOICE

The most famous trial in history is about to begin.

The judge is short and patrician with darting eyes and expensive clothes. His graying hair trimmed and face beardless. He is apprehensive, nervous about being thrust into a decision he can't avoid. Two soldiers lead him down the stone stairs of the fortress into the broad courtyard. Shafts of morning sunlight stretch across the stone floor.

As he enters, Syrian soldiers dressed in short togas yank themselves and their spears erect and stare straight ahead. The floor on which they stand is a mosaic of broad, brown, smooth rocks. On the floor are carved the games the soldiers play while awaiting the sentencing of the prisoner.

But in the presence of the procurator, they don't play.

A regal chair is placed on a landing five steps up from the floor. The magistrate ascends and takes his seat. The accused is brought into the room and placed below him. A covey of robed religious leaders follow, walk over to one side of the room, and stand.

Pilate looks at the lone figure.

"Doesn't look like a Christ," he mutters.

Feet swollen and muddy. Hands tan. Knuckles lumpy.

Looks more like a laborer than a teacher. Looks even less like a trouble-maker.

One eye is black and swollen shut. The other looks at the floor. Lower lip split and scabbed. Hair blood-matted to forehead. Arms and thighs streaked with crimson.

"Shall we remove the garment?" a soldier asks.

"No. It's not necessary."

It's obvious what the beating has done.

"Are you the king of the Jews?"

For the first time, Jesus lifts his eyes. He doesn't raise his head, but he lifts his eyes. He peers at the procurator from beneath his brow. Pilate is surprised at the tone in Jesus' voice.

"Those are your words."

"What should I do with Jesus, the one called the Christ?"

MATTHEW 27:22

Before Pilate can respond, the knot of Jewish leaders mock the accused from the side of the courtroom.

"See, he has no respect."

"He stirs the people!"

"He claims to be king!"

Pilate doesn't hear them. *"Those are your words."* No defense. No explanation. No panic. The Galilean is looking at the floor again.

Pilate looks at the Jewish leaders huddled in the corner across the court. Their insistence angers him. The lashes aren't enough. The mockery inadequate. *Jealous,* he wants to say to their faces, but doesn't. *Jealous buzzards, the whole obstinate lot of you. Killing your own prophets.*

Pilate wants to let Jesus go. *Just give me a reason,* he thinks, almost aloud. *I'll set you free.*

His thoughts are interrupted by a tap on the shoulder. A messenger leans and whispers. Strange. Pilate's wife has sent word not to get involved in the case. Something about a dream she had.

One hundred three

Pilate walks back to his chair, sits, and stares at Jesus. "Even the gods are on your side?" he states with no explanation.

He has sat in this chair before. It's a curule seat: cobalt blue with thick, ornate legs. The traditional seat of decision. By sitting on it Pilate transforms any room or street into a courtroom. It is from here he renders decisions.

How many times has he sat here? How many stories has he heard? How many pleas has he received? How many wide eyes have stared at him, pleading for mercy, begging for acquittal?

But the eyes of this Nazarene are calm, silent. They don't scream. They don't dart. Pilate searches them for anxiety . . . for anger. He doesn't find it. What he finds makes him shift again.

He's not angry with me. He's not afraid . . . he seems to understand.

Pilate is correct in his observation. Jesus is not afraid. He is not angry. He is not on the verge of panic. For he is not surprised. Jesus knows his hour and the hour has come.

Pilate is correct in his curiosity. Where, if Jesus is a leader, are his followers? What, if he is the Messiah, does he intend to do? Why, if he is a teacher, are the religious leaders so angry at him?

Pilate is also correct in his question. "What should I do with Jesus, the one called the Christ?"[1]

Perhaps you, like Pilate, are curious about this one called Jesus. You, like Pilate, are puzzled by his claims and stirred by his passions. You have heard the stories: God descending the stars, cocooning in flesh, placing a stake of truth in the globe. You, like Pilate, have heard the others speak; now you would like for him to speak.

What do you do with a man who claims to be God, yet hates religion?

What do you do with a man who calls himself the Savior, yet condemns systems? What do you do with a man who knows the place and time of his death, yet goes there anyway?

Pilate's question is yours. "What will I do with this man, Jesus?"

You have two choices.

You can reject him. That is an option. You can, as have many, decide that the idea of God becoming a carpenter is too bizarre—and walk away.

Or you can accept him. You can journey with him. You can listen for his voice amidst the hundreds of voices and follow him.

Pilate could have. He heard many voices that day—he could have heard Christ's. Had Pilate chosen to respond to this bruised Messiah, his story would have been different.

Pilate vacillates. He is a puppy hearing two voices. He steps toward one, then stops, and steps toward the other. Four times he tries to free Jesus, and four times he is swayed otherwise. He tries to give the people Barabbas; but they want Jesus. He sends Jesus to the whipping post; they want him sent to Golgotha. He states he finds nothing against this man; they accuse Pilate of violating the law. Pilate, afraid of who Jesus might be, tries one final time to release him; the Jews accuse him of betraying Caesar.

So many voices. The voice of compromise. The voice of expedience. The voice of politics. The voice of conscience.

One hundred five

And the soft, firm voice of Christ. "The only power you have over me is the power given to you by God."[2]

Jesus' voice is distinct. Unique. He doesn't cajole or plead. He just states the case.

Pilate thought he could avoid making a choice. He washed his hands of Jesus. He climbed on the fence and sat down.

But in not making a choice, Pilate made a choice.

Rather than ask for God's grace, he asked for a bowl. Rather than invite Jesus to stay, he sent him away. Rather than hear Christ's voice, he heard the voice of the people.

Legend has it that Pilate's wife became a believer. And legend has it that Pilate's eternal home is a mountain lake where he daily surfaces, still plunging his hands into the water seeking forgiveness. Forever trying to wash away his guilt . . . not for the evil he did, but for the kindness he didn't do.

THE GREATEST MIRACLE

*I*f the cross doesn't make sense on a common week full of common tasks, when does it make sense?

That is the beauty of the cross. It occurred in a normal week involving flesh-and-blood people and a flesh-and-blood Jesus.

Of all the weeks for Jesus to display his powers, his final week would be the one. A few thousand loaves or a few dozen healings would do wonders for his image. Better still, a few Pharisees struck dumb would make life simpler.

Don't just clean the temple, Jesus, pick it up and move it to Jericho. When the religious leaders mutter, make it rain frogs. And as you are describing the end times, split the sky and show everyone what you mean.

This is the week for razzle-dazzle. This is the hour for the incredible. You can silence them all, Jesus.

But he doesn't. Not in Jerusalem. Not in the upper room. Not on the cross.

The week, in many respects, is run-of-the-mill. Yes, it's festive, but its celebrations are due to the Passover, not Jesus. The crowds are large, but not because of the Messiah.

The two miracles Jesus performs aren't intended to draw a crowd. The

"People walked by... saying, 'You said you could destroy the Temple and build it again in three days.
So save yourself!
Come down from that cross, if you are really the Son of God!'"

MATTHEW 27:39-40

withered fig tree made a point, but turned few heads. The healed ear in the garden did a favor, but won no friends.

Jesus wasn't displaying his power.

It was an ordinary week.

An ordinary week packed with kids being dressed by impatient moms and dads hustling off to work. A week of dishes being washed and floors being swept.

Nature gave no clue that the week was different than any of the thousands before it or after it. The sun took its habitual route. The clouds puffed through the Judean sky. The grass was green and cattails danced in the wind.

Nature would groan before Sunday. The rocks would tumble before Sunday. The sky would put on a black robe before Sunday. But you wouldn't know that by looking at Monday, Tuesday, Wednesday, or Thursday. The week told no secrets.

The people gave no clue either. For most it was a week of anticipation; a weekend of festivities was arriving. Food to be bought. Houses to be cleaned. Their faces gave no forecast of the extraordinary—for they knew of none.

One would think the disciples would suspect something, but they don't. Corner them and probe their knowledge. They don't know. The only thing they know for sure is that his eyes seem more focused—he seems determined . . . about what they aren't sure.

Tell them that before Friday's dawn they will abandon their only hope, and they won't believe you. Tell them that Thursday night holds betrayal and denial, and they will scoff.

"Not us," they will boast.

For them this week is like any other. The disciples give no clue.

And most importantly, Jesus gives no clue. His water doesn't become wine. His donkey doesn't speak. The dead stay in the graves and those blind on Monday are still blind on Friday.

You'd think the heavens would be opened. You'd think trumpets would be sounding. You'd think angels would be summoning all the people of the world to Jerusalem to witness the event. You'd think that God himself would descend to bless his Son.

But he doesn't. He leaves the extraordinary moment draped in the ordinary. A predictable week. A week of tasks, meals, and crying babies.

A week which may be a lot like yours. Doubtful that anything spectacular has happened in your week. No great news, no horrible news. No earthquakes. No windfalls. Just a typical week of chores and children and checkout stands.

It was for the people of Jerusalem. On the edge of history's most remarkable hour was one of history's unremarkable weeks. God is in their city and most miss him.

Jesus could have used the spectacular to get their attention. Why didn't he? Why didn't he stun them with a loop-a-dee-loop or a double back-flip off the temple? When they demanded, "Crucify him!" why didn't he make their noses grow? Why is the miraculous part of Christ quiet this week? Why doesn't he do something spectacular?

No angelic shield protected his back from the whip. No holy helmet shielded his brow from the thorny crown. God crawled neck deep into the mire of humanity, plunged into the darkest cave of death, and emerged—alive.

Even when he came out, he didn't show off. He just walked out. Mary thought he was a gardener. Thomas had to have hands-on (or hands-in) proof. Jesus still ate, he still talked, he still broke bread with the Emmaus-bound disciples.

Do you see the point?

One hundred nine

God calls us in a real world. He doesn't communicate by performing tricks. He doesn't communicate by stacking stars in the heavens or reincarnating grandparents from the grave. He's not going to speak to you through voices in a cornfield or a little fat man in a land called Oz. There is about as much power in the plastic Jesus that's on your dashboard as there is in the Styrofoam dice on your rearview mirror.

It doesn't make a lick of difference if you are an Aquarius or a Capricorn or if you were born the day Kennedy was shot. God's not a trickster. He's not a genie. He's not a magician or a good luck charm or the man upstairs. He is, instead, the creator of the universe who is right here in the thick of our day-to-day world who speaks to you more through cooing babies and hungry bellies than he ever will through horoscopes, zodiac papers, or weeping Madonnas.

If you get some supernatural vision or hear some strange voice in the night, don't get too carried away. It could be God or it could be indigestion, and you don't want to misinterpret one for the other.

Nor do you want to miss the impossible by looking for the incredible. God speaks in our world. We just have to learn to hear him.

Listen for him amidst the ordinary.

Need affirmation of his care? Let the daily sunrise proclaim his loyalty.

Could you use an example of his power? Spend an evening reading how your body works.

Wondering if his Word is reliable? Make a list of the fulfilled prophecies in the Bible and promises in your life.

In the final week those who demanded miracles got none and missed the one. They missed the moment in which a grave for the dead became the throne of a king.

CHAPTER TWENTY-TWO

A PRAYER OF DISCOVERY

*L*ord?

Yes.

I may be stepping out of line by saying this, but I need to tell you something that's been on my mind.

Go ahead.

I don't like this verse: "My God, my God, why have you abandoned me?" It doesn't sound like you; it doesn't sound like something you would say.

Usually I love it when you speak. I listen when you speak. I imagine the power of your voice, the thunder of your commands, the dynamism in your dictates. That's what I like to hear.

> *"My God, my God, why have you abandoned me?"*
>
> MATTHEW 27:42, TEV

Remember the creation song you sang into the soundless eternity? Ah, now that's you. That was the act of a God!

And when you ordained the waves to splash and they roared, when you declared that the stars be flung and they flew, when you proclaimed that life be alive and it all began? . . . Or the whisper of breath into the clay-caked Adam? That was you at your best. That's the way I like to hear you. That's the voice I love to hear.

That's why I don't like this verse. Is that really you speaking? Are those words yours? Is that actually your voice? The voice which enflamed a bush, split a sea, and sent fire from heaven?

But this time, your voice is different.

Look at the sentence. There is a "why" at the beginning and a question mark at the end. You don't ask questions.

What happened to the exclamation point? That's your trademark. That's your signature closing. The mark as tall and strong as the words which precede it.

It's at the end of your command to Lazarus: "Come out!"[1]

It's there as you exorcise the demons: "Go!"[2]

It stands as courageously as you do as you walk on the waters and tell the followers: "Have courage!"[3]

Your words deserve an exclamation point. They are the cymbal clash of the finale, the cannon shot of victory, the thunder of the conquering chariots.

Your verbs form canyons and ignite disciples. Speak, God! You are the exclamation point of life itself. . . .

So, why the question mark hovering at the end of your words? Frail. Bent and bowed. Stooped as if weary. Would that you would straighten it. Stretch it. Make it stand tall.

And as long as I'm shooting straight with you—I don't like to see the word *abandon,* either. The source of life . . . abandoned? The giver of love . . . alone? The father of all . . . isolated?

Come on. Surely you don't mean it. Could deity feel abandoned?

Could we change the sentence a bit? Not much. Just the verb.

What would you suggest?

How about *challenge?* "My God, my God, why did you challenge me?" Isn't that better? Now we can applaud. Now we can lift banners for your dedication. Now we can explain it to our children. It makes sense now. You see, that makes you a hero. A hero. History is full of heroes.

And who is a hero but someone who survives a challenge.

Or, if that's not acceptable, I have another one. Why not *afflict*? "My God, my God, why did you afflict me?" Yes, that's it. Now you are a martyr, taking a stand for truth. A patriot, pierced by evil. A noble soldier who took the sword all the way to the hilt; bloody and beaten, but victorious.

Afflicted is much better than *abandoned*. You are a martyr. Right up there with Patrick Henry and Abraham Lincoln.

You are God, Jesus! You couldn't be abandoned. You couldn't be left alone. You couldn't be deserted in your most painful moment.

Abandonment. That is the punishment for a criminal. Abandonment. That is the suffering borne by the most evil. Abandonment. That's for the vile—not for you. Not you, the King of kings. Not you, the Beginning and the End. Not you, the One Unborn. After all, didn't John call you the Lamb of God?

What a name! That's who you are. The spotless, unblemished Lamb of God. I can hear John say the words. I can see him lift his eyes. I can see him smile and point at you and proclaim loud enough for all of Jordan to hear, "Behold, the Lamb of God. . . ."

And before he finishes his sentence, all eyes turn to you. Young, tan, robust. Broad shoulders and strong arms.

"Behold the Lamb of God. . . ."

Do you like that verse?

I sure do, God. It's one of my favorites. It's you.

What about the second part of it?

Hmmm, let me see if I remember. "Behold the Lamb of God who has come to take away the sins of the world."⁴ Is that it, God?

That's it. Think about what the Lamb of God came to do.

One hundred thirteen

"Who has come to take away the sins of the world." Wait a minute. "To take away the sins . . ." I'd never thought about those words.

I'd read them but never thought about them. I thought you just, I don't know, sent sin away. Banished it. I thought you'd just stood in front of the mountains of our sins and told them to begone. Just like you did to the demons. Just like you did to the hypocrites in the temple.

I just thought you commanded the evil out. I never noticed that you took it out. It never occurred to me that you actually touched it—or worse still that it touched you.

That must have been a horrible moment. I know what it's like to be touched by sin. I know what it's like to smell the stench of that stuff. Remember what I used to be like? Before I knew you, I wallowed in that mire. I didn't just touch sin, I loved it. I drank it. I danced with it. I was in the middle of it.

But why am I telling you? You remember. You were the one who saw me. You were the one who found me. I was lonely. I was afraid. Remember? "Why? Why me? Why has all this hurt happened?"

I know it wasn't much of a question. It wasn't the right question. But it was all I knew to ask. You see, God, I felt so confused. So desolate. Sin will do that to you. Sin leaves you shipwrecked, orphaned, adrift, aban—

Oh. My, goodness, God. Is that what happened? You mean sin did the same to you that it did to me?

I'm sorry. Oh, I'm so sorry. I didn't know. I didn't understand. You really were alone, weren't you?

Your question was real, wasn't it, Jesus? You really were afraid. You really were alone. Just like I was. Only, I deserved it. You didn't.

Forgive me, I spoke out of turn.

Sunday

CHAPTER TWENTY-THREE

THE HIDDEN TOMB

The road to Calvary was noisy, treacherous, and dangerous. And I wasn't even carrying a cross.

When I had thought of walking Christ's steps to Golgotha, I envisioned myself meditating on Christ's final hours and imagining the final turmoil. I was wrong.

Walking the Via Dolorosa is not a casual stroll in the steps of the Savior. It is, instead, an upstream struggle against a river of shoppers, soldiers, peddlers, and children.

"Watch your wallets," Joe told us.

I already am, I thought.

Joe Shulam is a Messianic Jew, raised in Jerusalem, and held in high regard by both Jew and Gentile. His rabbinic studies qualify him as a scholar. His archaeological training sets him apart as a researcher. But it is his tandem passion for the Messiah and the lost house of Israel which endears him to so many. We weren't with a guide, we were with a zealot.

And when a zealot tells you to guard your wallet, you guard your wallet.

Every few steps a street peddler would step in my path and dangle earrings or scarfs in my face. How can I meditate in this market?

For that is what the Via Dolorosa is. A stretch of road so narrow it bottlenecks body against body. When its sides aren't canyoned by the tall brick walls, they are lined with centuries-old shops selling everything from toys to dresses to turbans to compact discs. One section of the path is a butcher market. The smell turned my stomach and the sheep guts turned my eyes. Shuffling to catch up with Joe, I asked, "Was this street a meat market in the time of Christ?"

"It was," he answered. "To get to the cross he had to pass through a slaughterhouse."

It would be a few minutes before the significance of those words would register.

"Stay close," he yelled over the crowd. "The church is around the corner."

It'll be better at the church, I told myself.

Wrong again.

The Church of the Holy Sepulcher is 1700 years of religion wrapped around a rock. In A.D. 326 Empress Helena, the mother of Constantine the Great, came to Jerusalem in search of the hill on which Christ was crucified. Makarios, Bishop of Jerusalem, took her to a rugged outcropping outside of the northwestern wall of the city. A twenty-foot jagged cluster of granite upon which sat a Roman-built temple to Jupiter. Surrounding the hill was a cemetery made up of other walls of rock, dotted with stone-sealed graves.

Helena demolished the pagan temple and built a chapel in its place. Every visitor since has had the same idea.

The result is a hill of sacrifice hidden in ornateness. After entering a tall entrance to the cathedral and climbing a dozen stone steps, I stood at the front of the top of the rock. A glass case covers the tip and the tip is all that is visible. Beneath an altar is a gold-plated hole in which the cross supposedly was lodged. Three crucified icons with elongated faces hang on crosses behind the altar.

"He put Jesus' body in a new tomb that he had cut out of a wall of rock, and he rolled a very large stone to block the entrance of the tomb."

MATTHEW 27:60

Gold lanterns. Madonna statues. Candles and dim lights. I didn't know what to think. I was at once moved because of where I was standing and disturbed by what I was seeing.

I turned, descended the steps, and walked toward the tomb.

The traditional burial spot of Christ is under the same roof as the traditional Golgotha. To see it, you don't have to go outside; you do, however, have to use your imagination.

Two thousand years and a million tourists ago, this was a cemetery. Today it's a cathedral. The domes high above are covered with ornate paintings. I stopped and tried to picture it in its original state. I couldn't.

An elaborate sepulcher marks the traditional spot of Jesus' tomb. Forty-three lamps hang above the portal and a candelabra sits in front of it. It is solid marble, cornered with golden leaves.

An elevated stone path led into the doorway and a black-caped, black-bearded, black-hatted priest stood guard in front of it. His job was to keep the holy place clean. Fifty-plus people were standing in line to enter but he wouldn't let them. I didn't understand the purpose of the delay but I did understand the length of it.

"Twenty minutes. Twenty minutes."

The crowd mumbled. I mumbled. I came as close to the door as I could. The floor was inlaid with still more squares of marble and lanterns hung from the ceiling.

The sum total of the walk began to register with me. Holy road packed with peddlers. The cross hidden under an altar. The entrance to the tomb prohibited by a priest.

I had just muttered something about the temple needing another cleansing when I heard someone call. "No problem, come this way." It was

Joe Shulam speaking. What he showed us next I will never forget.

He took us behind the elaborate cupola, through an indiscreet entrance and guided us into a plain room. It was dark. It was musty. It was unkempt and dusty. Obviously not a place designed for tourists.

While our eyes adjusted, he began to speak. "Six or so of these have been found, but are seldom visited." Behind him was a small opening. It was a rock-hewn tomb. Four feet high at the most. The width about the same.

"Wouldn't it be ironic," he smiled as he spoke, "if this was the place? It is dirty. It is uncared for. It is forgotten. The one over there is elaborate and adorned. This one is simple and ignored. Wouldn't it be ironic if this was the place where our Lord was buried?"

I walked over to the opening and stooped like the apostle John did to see in the tomb. And, just like John, I was amazed at what I saw. Not the huge room I'd imagined in my readings, but a small room lit with a timid lamp.

"Go in," Joe urged. I didn't have to be told twice.

Three steps across the rock floor and I was at the other side. The low ceiling forced me to squat and lean against a cold, rough wall. My eyes had to adjust a second time. As they did, I sat in the silence, the first moment of silence that day. It began to occur to me where I was: in a tomb. A tomb which could have held the body of Christ. A tomb which could have encaved the body of God. A tomb which could have witnessed history's greatest moment.

"Five people could be buried here." Joe had entered and was at my side. A couple of my co-travelers were with him. "Two or three would be laid here on the floor. And two would be slid into the holes over here."

"God put himself in a place like this," someone said softly.

He did. God put himself in a dark, tight, claustrophobic room and allowed them to seal it shut. The Light of the World was mummied in cloth and shut in ebony. The Hope of humanity was shut in a tomb.

We didn't dare speak. We couldn't.

The elaborate altars were forgotten. The priest-protected sepulcher was a world away. What man had done to decorate what God came to do no longer mattered.

All I could see at that moment, perhaps more than any moment, was how far he had come. More than the God in the burning bush. Beyond the infant wrapped in a feed trough. Past the adolescent Savior in Nazareth. Even surpassing the King of kings nailed to a tree and mounted on a hill was this: God in a tomb.

Nothing is blacker than a grave, as lifeless as a pit, as permanent as the crypt.

But into the crypt he came.

The next time you find yourself entombed in a darkened world of fear, remember that. The next time pain boxes you in a world of horror, remember the tomb. The next time a stone seals your exit to peace, think about the empty, musty tomb outside of Jerusalem.

It's not easy to find. To see it you may have to get beyond the pressures of people demanding your attention. You may have to slip past the golden altars and ornate statues. To see it, you may even have to bypass the chamber near the priest and slip into an anteroom and look for yourself. Sometimes the hardest place to find the tomb is in a cathedral.

But it's there.

And when you see it, bow down, enter quietly, and look closely. For there, on the wall, you may see the charred marks of a divine explosion.

CHAPTER TWENTY-FOUR

SEE YOU
AT THE TABLE

"So what should I do with Jesus?" Pilate asked it first, but we've all asked it since.

It's a fair question. A necessary question. What do you do with such a man? He called himself God, but wore the clothes of a man. He called himself the Messiah, but never marshaled an army. He was regarded as king, but his only crown was of thorns. People revered him as regal, yet his only robe was stitched with mockery.

Small wonder Pilate was puzzled. How do you explain such a man?

One way is to take a walk. His walk. His final walk. And that is what we have done. We have followed his steps and stood in his shadow. From Jericho to Jerusalem. From the temple to the garden. From the garden to the trial. From Pilate's palace to Golgotha's cross. We have watched him walk—angrily into the temple, wearily into Gethsemane, painfully up the Via Dolorosa. And power-fully out of the vacated tomb.

"In the same way, the Son of Man did not come to be served. He came to serve others and to give his life as a ransom for many people."
MATTHEW 20:28

Hopefully, as you witnessed his walk, you have reflected on your own, for all of us have our own walk to Jerusalem. Our own path through hollow religion. Our own journey down the narrow path of rejection. And each of

One hundred twenty-three

us, like Pilate, must cast a verdict on Jesus.

Pilate heard the voice of the people and left Jesus to walk the road alone. Will we?

I hope that permanently planted in your soul is the moment the Father stirred you in the darkness and led you down the path to freedom. It's a memory like no other. For when he sets you free, you are free indeed.

Can I tell you my story?

A Bible class in a small West Texas town. I don't know what was more remarkable, that a teacher was trying to teach the book of Romans to a group of ten-year-olds or that I remember what he said.

The classroom was mid-sized, one of a dozen or so in a small church. My desk had carving on it and gum under it. Twenty or so others were in the room, though only four or five were taken.

We all sat at the back, too sophisticated to appear interested. Starched jeans. High-topped tennis shoes. It was summer and the slow-setting sun cast the window in gold.

The teacher was an earnest man. I can still see his flattop, his belly bulging from beneath his coat that he doesn't even try to button. His tie stops midway down his chest. He has a black mole on his forehead, a soft voice, and a kind smile. Though he is hopelessly out of touch with the kids of 1965, he doesn't know it.

His notes are stacked on a podium underneath a heavy black Bible. His back is turned to us and his jacket goes up and down his beltline as he writes on the board. He speaks with genuine passion. He is not a dramatic man, but tonight he is fervent.

God only knows why I heard him that night. His text was Romans chapter six. The blackboard was littered with long words and diagrams.

Somewhere in the process of describing how Jesus went into the tomb and came back out, it happened. The jewel of grace was lifted and turned so I could see it from a new angle . . . and it stole my breath.

I didn't see a moral code. I didn't see a church. I didn't see ten commandments or hellish demons. I saw my Father enter my dark night, awaken me from my slumber, and gently guide me—no, carry me—to freedom.

I said nothing to my teacher. I said nothing to my friends. I'm not sure I even said anything to God. I didn't know what to say. I didn't know what to do. But for all I didn't know there was one fact of which I was absolutely sure, I wanted to be with him.

I told my father that I was ready to give my life to God. He thought I was too young to make the decision. He asked what I knew. I told him Jesus was in heaven and I wanted to be with him. And for my dad, that was enough.

To this day I wonder if my love has ever been as pure as it was that first hour. I long for the certainty of my adorning faith. Had you told me that Jesus was in hell, I would have agreed to go. Public confession and baptism came naturally for me.

You see, when your Father comes to deliver you from bondage, you don't ask questions; you obey instructions. You take his hand. You walk the path. You leave bondage behind. And you never, never forget.

I pray you never forget your walk or his: Jesus' final walk from Jericho to Jerusalem. For it was this walk that promised you freedom.

His final walk through the temple of Jerusalem. For it was on this walk that he denounced hollow religion.

His final walk to the Mount of Olives. For it was there he promised to return and take you home.

And his final walk from Pilate's palace to Golgotha's cross. Bare, bloody feet struggling up a stony narrow path. But just as vivid as the pain of the beam against his raw back is his vision of you and him walking together.

He could see the hour he would come into your life, into your dark cabin to stir you out of your sleep and guide you to freedom.

But the walk isn't over. The journey isn't complete. There is one more walk that must be made.

"I will come back," he promised. And to prove it he ripped in two the temple curtain and split open the doors of death. He will come back.

"The one who has redeemed us has returned!" we will cry.

And the journey will end and we will take our seats at his feast . . . forever.

See you at the table.

NOTES

A WORD BEFORE

1. I've limited this book to the events in Christ's final week as recorded by Matthew.

CHAPTER ONE

1. Corinthians 1:26.

CHAPTER TWO

1. Matthew 20:18-19.
2. Acts 2:23.
3. Jeremiah 29:11.
4. Romans 8:1.
5. Hosea 11:9b.
6. Ephesians 3:18-19.

CHAPTER THREE

1. "D-Day Recalling Military Gamble that Shaped History," *Time,* 28 May 1984, 16.
2. Matthew 20:28.
3. For further reference consider the Book of Enoch, an intertestamental book completed sometime around 70 B.C. This ancient manuscript tells us what picture came to the minds of people when they heard the title "the Son of Man."
4. Matthew 19:28.
5. Matthew 24:30; Mark 13:26; Luke 17:26,30.
6. Matthew 26:64.
7. Mark 9:31.
8. Mark 9:32.
9. Matthew 20:28 isn't the only passage which speaks of the dual-

ism of God. He is the Lord "who shows mercy, who is kind . . . but he does not forget to punish guilty people" (Exodus 34:6,7). He is the only "good God." At the same time he is the "Savior" (Isaiah 45:21). He is equally "full of grace and truth" (John 1:14). He is the God who in wrath can remember mercy (Hebrews 3:2). In a precious insight Micah states to God, "You will not stay angry forever, because you enjoy being kind" (Micah 7:18). "God," states Paul, "is kind but also very strict" (Romans 11:22). He is able to "judge rightly and . . . make right any person who has faith in Jesus" (Romans 3:26).

CHAPTER FOUR

1. Luke 4:16, emphasis added.
2. Psalm 39:6, NIV.

CHAPTER FIVE

1. Matthew 26:10. Matthew waits until chapter 26 to tell a story which chronologically should appear in chapter 20. By referring to John's Gospel we see the anointing by Mary in Bethany occurred on Saturday night (John 12:1). Why does Matthew wait until so late to record the story? It appears that he sometimes elevates theme over chronology. The last week of Christ's life is a week of

bad news. Chapter 26 and 27 sing the woeful chorus of betrayal. First the leaders, then Judas, then the apostles, Peter, Pilate, and eventually all the people turn against Jesus. Perhaps with the desire to tell one good story of faith in the midst of so many ones of betrayal, Matthew waits until Matthew 26 to tell of Simon and Mary.
2. Matthew 26:13.

CHAPTER SIX

1. Matthew 21:2-3.
2. Matthew 5:41-42.

CHAPTER SEVEN

1. *Paul Harvey's For What It's Worth,* ed. Paul Harvey, Jr. (New York, N.Y.: Bantam Books, 1991), 118.
2. Mark 11:11.
3. Matthew 21:12-13.

CHAPTER EIGHT

1. It is obvious by comparing Matthew with Mark that the incident occurred on two days. Part on Monday and part on Tuesday. The cleansing of the temple occurred between these two parts.

By combining Matthew and Mark we see that the cursing of the tree took place on Monday and the commentary occurred on Tuesday. There is no conflict. One writer is topical and the other chronological. Each has it advantages. (See William Hendricksen, *The Gospel of Matthew* [Grand Rapids, Mich.: Baker Book House, 1973], 773).

2. Matthew 21:21.

3. Matthew 21:22.

CHAPTER NINE

1. Matthew 21:33-45.

2. Matthew 22:1-14.

3. 2 Samuel 7:15.

4. Matthew 21:43.

5. Acts 13:46.

6. Matthew 12:24.

CHAPTER TEN

1. Isaiah 1:18.

2. Isaiah 55:1.

3. Matthew 11:28.

4. Matthew 22:4.

5. Mark 1:17.

6. John 7:37.

7. Matthew 21:28-32.

8. Matthew 22:1-14.

9. Revelation 3:20.

10. Hebrews 9:27, RSV.

CHAPTER ELEVEN

1. Matthew 22:42.

CHAPTER TWELVE

1. Matthew 23:8-12.

2. Matthew 23:8.

3 Matthew 23:9.

4. Matthew 23:10.

CHAPTER THIRTEEN

1. John 16:33.

2. Matthew 24:5.

3. Matthew 24:6.

4. Matthew 24:7-8.

5. Matthew 24:9.

6. *The Wall Street Journal,* 15 January 1992, A-P1.

7. Matthew 24:13.

8. Matthew 24:14.

9. Acts 2:5.

10. Matthew 24:14.

CHAPTER FOURTEEN

1. Matthew 24:36.

2. Matthew 25:1-13.

3. Matthew 25:14-30.

4. Matthew 25:31-46.

CHAPTER FIFTEEN

1. Matthew 24:45-51.1

2. Matthew 25:1-13.

3. Matthew 25:14-30.

4. Matthew 24:42.

5. Matthew 25:31.

6. Matthew 24:44.

7. Acts 1:11, NIV.

8. Hebrews 9:28.

9. 1 Thessalonians 5:2, NIV.

10. Matthew 25:32-33.

11. Matthew 25:41.

12. 1 Thessalonians 5:9, NEB.

13. Hebrews 9:27.

14. Matthew 7:24-27.

15. Matthew 7:13-14.

16. Paul Lee Tan, *Encyclopedia of 7007 Illustrations* (Rockville, M.D.: Assurance Publishers, 1979), 1086.

CHAPTER SIXTEEN

1. Matthew 25:35-36.

2. Hebrews 11:6b.

3. Matthew 25:40.

4. *San Antonio Express-News,* 3 April 1991, 2.

CHAPTER SEVENTEEN

1. Matthew 26:18.

2. John 13:5.

3. A sacrament is a gift from the Lord to his people.

4. A sacrifice is a gift of the people to the Lord.

5. There are sacrificial moments during the Supper. We offer up prayers, confessions, and thanksgivings as sacrifice. But they are sacrifices of thanksgiving for a salvation received, not sacrifices of service for a salvation desired. We don't say, "Look at what I've done." We instead, in awe, watch God and worship what he has done.

6. Romans 8:34.

7. Luke 12:37.

CHAPTER EIGHTEEN

1. John 17:20-21.

CHAPTER NINETEEN

1. Matthew 26:46.

2. Matthew 26:50.

3. Matthew 26:15.

4. Matthew 26:48-49.

5. Matthew 26:49.

6. James 1:2.

7. Matthew 26:64.

8. Hebrews 13:5.

CHAPTER TWENTY

1. Matthew 27:22.

2. John 19:11.

CHAPTER TWENTY-TWO

1. John 11:43.

2. Matthew 8:32.

3. Matthew 14:27.

4. John 1:29.